C000272208

Baggage

Baggage
A Book of Leavings

Victoria Field

Francis
Boutle
Publishers

First published by
Francis Boutle Publishers
272 Alexandra Park Road
London N22 7BG
Tel/Fax: (020) 8889 7744
Email: info@francisboutle.co.uk
www.francisboutle.co.uk

Baggage: A Book of Leavings © Victoria Field, 2016

All rights reserved.
No part of this book may be reproduced, stored
in a retrieval system, or transmitted, in any form
or by any means, electronic, mechanical
photocopying or otherwise without the prior
permission of the publishers.

ISBN 978 0 9935344 3 0

Printed and bound in Great Britain by TJ International Ltd, Padstow

Contents

Acknowledgements

I am grateful to Tim and Jane Jordan for our long friendship, and for giving me the final nudge to make this journey.

Thank you to Paul Dodgson, Sara Maitland and Nikki Wilkins for their generous encouragement and helpful comments on earlier versions of *Baggage*, and to Kay Cotton and Sylvia Miles for their warm hospitality.

Thanks are due to the following for permission to reproduce poems:

Alfred A. Knopf Inc for 'Island' by Langston Hughes from *The Collected Poems of Langston Hughes* (Knopf, 1994)

Bloodaxe Books and Jane Hirshfield for 'Three Times My Life Has Opened' from Jane Hirshfield, *Each Happiness Ringed by Lions: Selected Poems* (Bloodaxe Books, 2005) www.bloodaxebooks.com

Francis Boutle and D.M. Thomas for 'Morning Coffee' from *Two Countries* (Francis Boutle, 2011)

Of my own poems, 'Vague Memory', 'Bardsey Island' and 'Early' were published in 'Olga's Dreams' (fal, 2004) and 'For Destruction, Water' in *Raceme* magazine (September 2015)

And so they stayed there for fourteen days in that country, and there she had great happiness, both bodily and spiritually, high devotion, and many loud cryings at the memory of our Lord's Passion, with abundant tears of compassion.

The Book of Margery Kempe (1438)

Every poem breaks a silence.

Adrienne Rich

Prologue

I'm packing my rucksack. It's small, larger than a day pack, but nowhere near as big as a back-packer's pack. First in goes my new sleeping bag. I'm in love with my sleeping bag. In its tight little stuff-bag, it's tiny, barely bigger than a small loaf of bread. When I saw it in Millets, it seemed like a miracle. The shop assistant shook it free and it flew into the room like a shiny grey cloud, all softness and warmth. I didn't believe it could be squashed back into its sack but she assured me, don't give up, just keep going, squeeze, stuff, squeeze, and as we chatted, she pushed fistfuls of cloud into the impossibly small sack. And yes, eventually, the cloud had gone and we were left with the solid little cylinder. All this magic was mine for just £20.

The next items are bulky and bothersome and carry a freight of anxiety – tampons, sanitary towels, pain killers – I'll have my period somewhere along the Way. I know that the hostels can be primitive and I've no idea what the toilets and showers will be like. As I approach middle age, my periods have become heavier and the possibility of shame and embarrassment looms large. I realise how much I value a private bathroom and think of how one important barrier to girls' education in countries like Pakistan and India is the simple lack of toilet facilities in schools and colleges. Here in Cornwall, 'protection' is inexpensive if voluminous in my little pack. I feel pleased, though, that these items won't come back with me and at some stage, I'll have that space back in the rucksack.

Clothes. I have a heap on the living room table. On each packing and repacking, the pile gets smaller. Three seems an appropriate number for knickers, socks and t-shirts, a holy trinity of wash, wear and spare. One jumper, one raincoat, one hat. Pyjamas present a dilemma but in the end I decide that sleep will be one of the pleasures of the trip and I'll sleep better appropriately dressed. Indulgently, I add a pillow case so I don't come into contact with smelly old pillows. One pair of trousers, one pair of shorts.

The challenge of toiletries is to take just enough. Some of it's non-negotiable: toothpaste, soap, shampoo, sun screen, all in satisfyingly tiny bottles but a dissatisfying amount of plastic. Where I indulge, though, is in a whole series of unguents for my feet: cracked heel cream, arnica for bruises, refreshing gel, tea tree for infections, blister plasters. Then accessories: a small towel, face flannel, wet-wipes, hairbrush. Precisely counted vitamin pills.

One of the differences between walking as a hobby or a sport, and the tradition of pilgrimage, is that there's a whole industry devoted to making the former easier on the body, whereas the latter is supposed to be difficult. Bodily discomfort is part of the process. This is made most manifest in the question of boots. My current pair is a couple of years old, very cheap and somewhat nasty. They aren't particularly worn but have an unpleasant aroma when wet so I keep them in the garage. I suspect it's as much the stench of misery from the Chinese factory where they were made as my malodorous feet. People keep advising me to invest in a 'good pair of boots' so I do some research, get depressed at the three figure prices and the amount of effort by scientific minds which might have been put to better use elsewhere. A practice walk along a challenging stretch of the Cornish Coast Path of 28 miles in a day and a half, left me unable to move. My back muscles had been pulled tight by over-worked quadriceps and hamstrings, but my feet in their cheap boots were unscathed. They emerged from my wet socks white and scoured like a statue, totally free of blisters or bruises. So, I wear my old boots and pack a pair of chunky pink sandals to let my feet breath in the evening.

Almost there. A notebook – slim moleskin and two Pilot V5 pens. Three would have been nice, I'm fetishistic about them and buy them by the box, but three suggests a lack of faith, an over-abundance which means, paradoxically, I'm more likely to lose them. I reluctantly pack two. Camera. Two books I'm willing to discard – a minor novel by Cornish Nobel Laureate, William Golding and 'Colloquial Spanish' which has followed me around since my A' Level almost thirty years ago.

The pack is full. I pull in the drawstring at the top and tighten the various straps which surround it like ivy on a tree. It weighs about seven kilos. I slide a plastic wallet into the pocket on one side, containing my passport, e-tickets for flights and electronic booking confirmations for a hotel in Madrid and trains across Spain. Into the other pocket goes a small metal flask for cold water or hot drinks. Around my waist, a money belt with 500 euros and £100 in notes, a pretty little purse for coins, a debit card, my ticket for the sleeper train from Truro to London. A lipstick.

I'm ready. But it's a chilly end-of-summer evening, so I unpack the rucksack and retrieve my jumper, put it on and repack, more efficiently this time, so the drawstring and straps are more easily tightened. I stand back and look at the pack sitting in the middle of the table, curving round its plastic frame like a stooping old person or a crescent moon. I put a Cornish gold cross around my neck – a Christmas present from my husband before we parted and little silver stars in my ears. I wear a ring belonging to one of my grandmothers.

My baggage. And of course the realisation that wherever I take it, my body and my history will come too. So I set off, with my forty six years, my hopes and regrets, my memories, my broken marriage, my losses and enthusiasms, my short legs and large breasts, my small feet and curly hair, my rusty Spanish and love of walking, my excitement and apprehension, my crappy boots and gorgeous sleeping bag.

Chapter One

Beginnings and endings

Leon to Mazarife, 26th September

I'm lost already. Although León's full of pilgrims wandering around with rucksacks, I'm not yet one of them. I'm just a person who happens to be carrying a backpack. It isn't just a case of my readiness to fight giants and hobgoblins, I need my *credencial*, a so-called Pilgrim's Passport, to be shown at hostels, cafes, restaurants, churches or other places authorised to issue a *sello*, a stamp. My *credencial* will be the evidence that I've followed the *camino*, the Way, from León to Santiago. I can't start without it.

Someone shows me a little map in a guidebook and it seems the Oficina de Peregrinos is back along the *camino* at a junction on the way out of town to the east. I walk along the old streets of León, through medieval gates in the city walls, to where the ancient centre gives way to modern urban sprawl. There are shops selling walking gear but no Pilgrim's Office. I'm frustrated – I want to get going, but there's no point beginning without the *credencial*. I won't be able to stay in the hostels, eat in the pilgrim's restaurants nor receive, at the end, my *compostela*, my indulgence, my Access-All-Areas pass to heaven. I double-back and go forward again, ask in shops, ask passers-by, all to no avail. I have a gander at the cathedral and pester an official. Where's the Pilgrim's Office? No one knows. They should surely know in the cathedral. Always, there's a 'they' to blame.

Eventually, someone tells me that there's an office issuing *credenciales* in the hostel that's also a monastery in the middle of the old town, down a little alley. It's easy to find and I kick myself that I walked straight past it on my determined march out of town an hour earlier.

It's still only just ten in the morning and the gates to the courtyard are closed and locked. Peering through a barred window gives me my first glimpse of a hostel dormitory. It's unwelcoming, like an old-fashioned orphanage or psychiatric ward, except worse, as the beds are bunks, too close together and metal-framed with grimy, sagging mattresses. I wait, leaning against a window sill, fresh-faced and wide-eyed in my clean, first-day-of-walking clothes, as slow-moving people with tatty rucksacks roll up. They aren't friendly and look exhausted with closed expressions on tired faces. Checking in to a hostel so early in the morning suggests they won't have walked far that day and I wonder if some are unwell. León though, is a big city, a good place to pause for a rest and a look around for those that have come a long way on foot.

Eventually, an official from the monastery comes through the giant arch and unlocks the gate. He's a paunchy, relaxed-looking man, in an open collared shirt, doesn't look like a monk, and tells us we can go up and either check in for the night, or in my case, collect my documents.

I'm at the front of the queue and suddenly my hurriedness fades away and I'm awed by the process that's beginning. Even though I've hurtled through airports and railway stations from Cornwall to Spain, the centuries fall away and I'm not 'me' any more but a pilgrim, just one of the millions who have passed through this city and, probably, this very doorway, as the monastery has been a hostel since medieval times. I fantasise I've come from Cornwall on a dangerous boat from Fowey to Bordeaux, rather than on planes and trains through the heat and pollution of London and Madrid.

Margery Kempe, an illiterate, and intensely vocal, visionary may have stood on these very stairs. A friend describes her as the 'patron saint of the mid-life crisis'. She began having visions and devoting her life to pilgrimage after the birth of her fourteenth child and went to Santiago in 1417. It took her days to make the sea crossing from Bristol to the North coast of Spain. It was a perilous undertaking in those times, both because of the rough weather across the Bay of Biscay, and the banditry among fellow pilgrims. Margery had additional problems as her devotions often took the form of loud crying and understandably, she'd become a notorious nuisance to other pilgirms. Her Book, the earliest surviving autobiography in English, was dictated by her in old age and throughout, she refers to herself in the third person as 'this creature'. Margery relates how 'she had been told that if they had any storm, they would throw her into the sea, for they said it would be because of her: and they said the ship was the worse for her being in it'. Fortunately, her prayers were answered, there were no storms on her crossing and, she relates, 'our Lord granted her her boon ... sent fair wind and weather, so that they reached Santiago on the seventh day.'

It's taken me thirty six hours to reach León from Cornwall. Storms were unlikely to hold me up in a mild September, nor was there much risk of being thrown out of a plane or train by fellow pilgrims. A day and a half, most of it comfy with readily available food and drink, isn't much of a journey by medieval standards but it's still longer than most A to B trips by air.

I can't lay claim to Margery's commitment or depth of visions, but I, too, am a creature searching for God and meaning by travelling. I'm part of a tradition that's enjoying a massive revival. The practice of making pilgrimages from Britain and Ireland dwindled after the Reformation, but now the numbers of pilgrims from countries all over the world, are increasing steadily each year. In 1989, around two thousand people were awarded a *compostela*. the document confirming that at least the last hundred kilometres of the route to Santiago have been completed on foot, or the last two hundred by bicycle or on horseback. Twenty years later, in 2009, the number is around a hundred thousand and the estimate for 2010, a Jubilee Year when St James' Feast Day, 25th July, falls on a Sunday, is two hundred thousand. The numbers seem high but are still only a fraction of the estimated half a million a year who walked to Santiago in the 11th and 12th centuries. The trend though is steadily upward.

The reasons for this new interest in the Camino de Santiago, are many. Every year, books get written and translated, feature films are made, television personalities give interviews, air travel is cheap and the internet gives detailed information about everything. Yet, standing in this building, with its cold scent of stone and hardly anything in the way of electrical or plastic paraphernalia, there's little to tell me I'm in any particular century at all. Margery's contemporaries, in all their flea-invested garb, could materialise at any point. And the matter of human locomotion, simply putting one foot in front of the other until you get there, hasn't changed at all in the intervening six hundred years.

The receptionist sits on a low chair at a low table, so even I, a short

person, tower over him. He's young and tiny and seems to have had polio
or some other disease that has left him crooked and slowed his
movements. He's writing in a giant ledger. When I say I have come for a
credencial rather than to check-in to sleep, he heaves himself to his feet
with a sigh, lurches with enormous effort across the little office to take
forms from a drawer behind him, then motions me to complete them in
a canteen area opposite. He's extremely polite, courtly almost, and very,
very slow. This too dissipates my feeling at wanting to get going, to get
started. Pilgrims have been coming to this monastery for so long that our
contemporary focus on hurrying seems rather silly. It's taken me forty six
years to get here, why the rush, why the irritation?

I tick the box saying that I'm doing the pilgrimage for religious
reasons, rather than 'other', and that I will abide by the code required. It's
a basic Christian do-as-you-would-be-done-by list of rules to respect the
rest of other pilgrims, to demand nothing by right and to be grateful for
all help received. The document folds out concertina-fashion, with
spaces for the *sellos* to be collected along the way. It's old-fashioned-
looking, reminiscent of the Youth Hostel membership cards of my teens
in which I collected the exotic stamps of Beachy Head, Crockham Hill
and other hostels I could reach by bicycle in a weekend, or my first black-
backed passport with its intriguing and colourful visas and entry stamps
to countries in Eastern Europe in a world that no longer exists.

I take the completed forms back to the tiny man. With great care and a
proper fountain pen, he enters my name, passport number and nationality into the giant ledger and stamps my *credencial* before wishing me
'Buen Camino'. I'm moved to tears, as if I've just been baptised or
awarded some unexpected prize, and stupidly ask how much it costs. It
feels like a philistine twentieth-first century question. He says it's 'by
donation' and I put an extravagant amount in the box but it doesn't feel
enough. What would be the right amount to pay for pilgrim credentials
and all that goes with them – this long route, its cathedrals, mountains
and monasteries, the tradition of hospitality, the memories and stories of
the millions of people who've walked it, their prayers and tears and hopes
and fears?

Putting a figure on things is something I've always found hard. You
and I never sorted out that side of our defunct marriage. The solicitor
who made it very easy for me to dissolve our marriage, was keen to

finalise the financial side of things and asked me, 'Well, what do you need?'. I couldn't answer. I couldn't put a price on getting a sense of self back, or developing an understanding of what had gone on. She pressed me, and I remembered a divorcing friend's inventory of 'needs' which included weekly hair-dressing, a new car every year, holidays, therapy and decent clothes. I couldn't imagine myself in those terms and genuinely didn't know. 'Nothing at the moment.' She looked at me as if I was an idiot and said, 'Well, let's leave it open but I advise you sort it out as soon as possible.' Strangely, and also wisely, it seems that the question of what divorcing spouses might need from each other stays open even when one of them dies. It closes automatically for one who remarries – which you did quickly – as if marriage is a way of instantly meeting every need, not just those to do with money or property. I need to understand what happened between us, to find a story or create a story out of the journey we made together. I need to walk 212 miles to Santiago, think and write it all down.

I step out from the cool monastery into bright sunshine. I've officially begun. Unofficially, I started well before I was issued with my *credencial*. Already, I've travelled from Cornwall on the sleeper train where the new carriages have video facilities. I snuggled into the little bunk and watched Doc Martin with its familiar Port Isaac setting and Cornish actor friends playing goony local characters. Already, I've experienced the sleeper breaking down and having to change trains in the small hours in Bristol, listening to furious passengers who were going to miss their early flights from Heathrow. Already, being on a mid-day flight, I've had time to walk from Paddington across Kensington Gardens to Earls Court, trying out different rhythms, with my rucksack alternately loose or tightly strapped. I sat in the sun near Palace Gate, enjoying a bright autumn morning in London and had a picnic breakfast on a bench. Already in transit, I was more at one with London's rough sleepers than the professional dog-walkers, filipino nannies and wealthy locals, jogging and stretching with their personal trainers.

Already, I've spent Friday night in Madrid, after escaping the labyrinthine airport terminal, where each cavernous marble and glass atrium led into yet another one and the whole building was a version of Dante's Inferno. I sweltered on the Metro to the grotty hotel I'd booked on the Gran Vía. I've had tapas in a buzzing bar, eaten farmed trout in a pavement cafe near the Plaza Mayor and passed drug dealers and under-age prostitutes as I walked back to my hotel. All night, Madrid partied and roared.

Already, I've got up before dawn and taken the Metro to Charmatín, sharing the compartment with revellers, who, at 6am, were just heading home. Their mingled breath filled the carriage with a heavy smell of nicotine and alcohol and many of them were asleep, heads nodding to the judder of the train or lolling on the shoulders of boyfriends and girl-friends. Already, I've passed the security check to get on to the pristine train to León, already I've clocked how late the sun rises. Spain, in spite of being so far west, keeps Central European time. Madrid, like my home town of Falmouth is five degrees west from Greenwich, yet is two hours ahead. It seemed like mid-morning when the dawn eventually revealed a new kind of countryside as mist lifted from farms and villages.

Or did the journey start even earlier with emails from people who were planning to 'do' the *camino*? Was it the stories of Anne Marie, my American friend, once living in Falmouth by way of Moldova, who's walked the *camino* five or six times? Or was it meeting a man in Greece a couple of years ago who mined his experiences for a novel that's also about his various selves? Or was it much earlier, when I took to Spanish at school like a *pato* to *agua*, first heard of Santiago and knew at the age of thirteen I wanted to go there? Or was it in my genes, always a walker from the age of two when I refused the pushchair, insisting on toddling beside my mum for the mile or so to the shops, from Raynes Park to Wimbledon, and back? Was it the growing coherence and importance of religion in my life that made me want to experience a Christian tradition going back to the journey of the Magi, or to follow an even more ancient impulse such as prompted Abraham to leave his home in Ur for Canaan? It may have been all of these, or none of them, just the strange motives that are unknown to ourselves to which we later attribute logical provenance.

Perhaps the desire to go on pilgrimage is a universal aspect of being human, one that the medievals understood well, the need to walk both away from, and towards, what's important, what poet, James Harpur describes as the 'irresistible prompting to exchange the familiar with the strange'. It may be the answer to a sense that the present environment is no longer serving us well, that there are questions that can only be answered, or even asked, far from home.

I don't know quite when I started my pilgrimage, I do know when our marriage finally ended. It wasn't when the divorce papers arrived, but the day a removal van came to our home, rendering it once again, your home. You too realised, for the first time maybe, that it really was over and you sat at our kitchen table, head in your hands, crying.

People say women identify particularly strongly with their houses and in Gestalt psychology, dreams of houses are said to be dreams about the self. You though, atypically of your sex, were especially merged with your home, wearing your house as closely as an outer skin. I sometimes thought of you as a snail, because it fitted you so well and away from it, you seemed naked and vulnerable. Getting you to go anywhere was always an effort. The outside world is hostile to smokers, your bad back was intolerant of journeys by car or plane, parties or plays can be dull and difficult to leave. Also, as I've discovered myself, simple gravity keeps people stuck down in the long peninsula of Cornwall. It's hard to resist the inertia, to get out and go, as the Cornish say, up-country.

In contrast, I've always been a traveller, identifying with my merchant seaman father. Unlike you, I've never anchored myself in a house. I've twice bought and renovated a house, and each time, I soon moved on, renting it out and upping sticks for other horizons. For most of my adult life, I've lived in rented flats and houses so my possessions aren't many and the van wasn't large.

I was already living away from our marital home where I'd felt like Jane Eyre to your Mr Rochester. Like Thornfield Hall, although on a smaller scale, there was a gloom over your granite house even on a sunny day. A long, narrow converted coach house it originally belonged to a nearby manor which had burned down. It always felt wrongly placed to me, sitting oddly diagonal across a hillside. The long side, with its many windows and pretty French doors replacing the stable openings, faces uphill towards a new housing estate, blocked off by a hedge of brooding leylandii. Only two windows, those of the living room and that of your upstairs study, both on the narrow side of the house, overlook the valley and the colourful garden with its magnificent beech tree.

Your girlfriend must have already moved in but I don't remember her being there that day. There was evidence, though, of a stranger in residence with unfamiliar items that might pass for antiques dotted around the house. It looked like the kind of dusty clutter which builds up

in the houses of elderly people who haven't moved in decades and is opti-
mistically put up for sale at boot fairs. In retrospect, of course, I see it was
a marking out of territory by the new, would-be woman of the house.
Your elder son was staying upstairs in the spare room and made a brief
appearance with a stricken look on his face as I stomped around with
cardboard boxes.

I was removing my possessions and by implication myself. I was no
longer possessed by you. I no longer possessed you. We were severing our
vows. I read that some Benedictine monks are encouraged to list their
possessions at the beginning of Lent and then, after the forty days, decide
which ones they really want in their lives. With the sheer burden of stuff
in a typical modern home, it would take most of Lent just to make the list.
Strangely, though, even now, I could probably identify most of the possessions I moved into your home when we married and which were now
being carried out by the kindly father and son team to the removal van.
They would take them up along the A30, the main artery along the granite
spine of Cornwall, to the remote farmhouse on Bodmin Moor where I'd
rented a wing to rest and recuperate from the pain of this severing.

The packing up took a while. Somehow, I thought I'd make a quick
get-away, an hour at most, but the process lasted most of the morning. I'd
already stacked my pictures against a downstairs wall and boxed up my
books, but my desk and bookshelves needed dismantling to be got
through various doors, and the antique pine dresser, given to us by my
mum as a wedding present, had to be handled with care. There was then
the skilled business of packing the van so that everything went in, yet
didn't move around too much.

I was aware I hadn't thoroughly checked the bookshelves in the dining
room, where I'd amalgamated our poetry and psychology books.
Alexander Pushkin, on his deathbed in his study at 12, Moika in
Petersburg, after being fatally wounded in a duel, waved at his bookshelves saying, 'Farewell, my friends.' You're a skilled and reverential
translator of Russian poetry and at the beginning of our affair, would
quote Pushkin constantly. That my friends and your friends were
mingled in the bookcases seemed a happy metaphor for marriage, and I
liked seeing our two copies of, say, Freud's *Interpretation of Dreams*, and
many poetry collections, often in different editions, published years
apart, sitting side-by-side on the shelf.

You'd acquired many of your books when you were a student in the 1950s and others were dedicated to you by poets long dead. I envied you your traditional Oxford English degree that began with Beowulf and finished somewhere towards the end of the nineteenth century. You continued that conversation of letters, both through your teaching, your love of twentieth-century poets and later through your own writing. Your elder son is a commercially successful novelist and your other children too are talented writers. In the early days, before we married, you often mentioned that you wanted a protégée and that you'd said to Anthony Clare, when you sat 'In the Psychiatrist's Chair' back in 1990, that you also wanted to know 'a great love'.

I'm not sure I was either – perhaps in your head in the beginning, certainly not then as I irritably snatched books from the shelves and slotted them spine up into the banana boxes I'd collected in Asda. As I prepared to put us asunder, to abandon you and all we share, I was distracted by picking up one of your treasures – a hardback notebook full of dedications from famous poets of the sixties. When you were lecturing at a teacher training college in Hereford, you invited poets to come and give readings and would get them to sign this book. You would tell anecdotes about Anne Sexton visiting you with her biographer in tow and dismissing you at her hotel bedroom door once she'd taken her medication. Ted Hughes, devoid of small talk, apparently read from his work without introduction or justification and reduced the women of Hereford to weak-kneed girls. George Barker was on some kind of residency but appeared only twice, and then drunk, while collecting a generous fee. One evening, before we married, we were at a hilarious dinner at a literature festival in Devon. Poets a generation younger than you exclaimed in delight, 'You kissed Anne Sexton! You actually kissed Anne Sexton!' as if you'd touched the robes of Christ or seen for yourself the stone rolled away from the tomb.

Picking out my books was a bit like sharing friends after divorce – except with the books, I had a choice of which to leave and which to take with me. Our real friends were different and made their own minds up. One couple invited you and your new wife to dinner, but never me, another sent a card saying, 'We'll always be friends with both of you' but I don't hear from them for years. There are others who told me, 'Thank goodness, we can see more of you – he was always so difficult'. So I give up trying to be absolute and leave behind not just some of my books, but an antique chair you find comfortable, some of the ornaments we were given as wedding presents and a few things I superstitiously hide around the house so that, no matter what, I will never be completely gone. Slipping an icon of Our Lady of Kazan under our mattress in an attempt to freak out your new girlfriend was going a bit far, but *in extremis* we're all crazy and believe in magic.

The chair is where you sat to watch television in the evenings, important rugby or cricket matches during the day, feeding bits of Carr's Table Water biscuits to the dog as you alternately, or even simultaneously, snacked and smoked. You probably still sit there smoking in front of the television in the evenings, although you've been on a diet and the dog died some years ago, so I am guessing it's without the biscuits.

At last! No more planes and trains, no more circumlocutions around the city – I have my *credencial* and am ready to go. It's disconcertingly easy to find the route out of town, signs and arrows are everywhere. My experience contrasts profoundly with Colm Tóibín's account of walking out of León in the early '90s when he gets lost several times, and when often the only signs of the way to go were bits of yellow string tied in bushes. Here in spick and span León, in the new millennium, there are neat little scallop shell symbols everywhere I look, so the going is more than easy.

I set off at a cracking pace. I know today is going to be the most dreary in terms of scenery, with several miles of suburbs and industrial estates before getting into the countryside. León city centre is beautiful with fountains, ancient buildings and serene squares but I walk on past them all. The gigantic palace is now a *parador*, a state-run luxury hotel, and I vow to stay there another time but today leave it behind. It doesn't matter that I haven't looked at León properly. I am here to walk and think, not sight-see. There'll always be the option of returning by car or bus some time in the future to look at the monuments. Years ago, someone gave me an article by Jan Morris on the 'craft of travel' and one of her maxims was that it's best to do just one thing when on a trip, not to combine incompatible activities. So choose to sunbathe, or look at old churches or drink cocktails – rather than try to do everything. So here, in Spain, my task is to walk, think, heal. The history can wait.

Our holidays together were a model of that practice. Every winter, we'd go on a package holiday to some bland and pleasant resort. There were just two requirements – cheap cigarettes and enough sun for us to sit and eat fish by a pretty harbour where boats bob and chink in a warm breeze. Islands, always islands. We met on Skyros, one of our first trips away was to Tobago, later we went to Madeira, Martinique, Mallorca, Cyprus, Tenerife and several times to Lanzarote. Even Cornwall is almost an island – the River Tamar slices it off from Devon with only a few miles of marshy fields keeping this long-fingered bit of land attached to Britain rather than drifting off towards Avalon and the Atlantic. A few of our island trips were work but most were pure holiday. I'd drive the hire car – a nifty Renault Clio or similar and you would sort-of map read. We'd inevitably have an argument during the first hour as I tried to find our way out of a city or the airport, crunching the gears and fumbling for indicators. I'd blame you for missing a turning or not getting us into the right lane, for not even *trying* to concentrate. Then, once we'd got going in the right direction, I'd relax, we'd have the windows down, you leaning out with a cigarette, me enjoying the waft of smoke on herb-scented warm air and the pleasure of bowling along an open road.

We'd spend the days, driving around, stopping for coffee, stopping for lunch, stopping for tea before quiet evenings in the hotel, reading our books over gin and tonic on the balcony, taking our time over dinner, early to bed. I'd sometimes go alone for a swim – as a Cornishman born inland in the mining district of Redruth, you distrusted the sea and couldn't swim. I don't think you were frightened so much as you couldn't be bothered with all that changing, getting wet and so on. On Tobago, where we stayed in a dispiriting hotel with ant-infested rooms and no air-conditioning, a friend and I persuaded you into the pool to cool down. You allowed yourself to be supported by us linking arms to make a raft and soon you were weightless and swimming before you suddenly remembered that this really wasn't for you. You stood up in the tepid water and quickly made your way out of the unfamiliar medium.

On those winter holidays, we generally wouldn't talk to other people, being happy in our bubble of hire car and book-reading and I remember our own conversation being easy most of the time. The bland sunniness of the islands was a balm and the lack of things to do, especially for bookish, unsporty people like us, meant no pressure to do them. Rather, there was a short and predictable list that comprised the 'must-sees'

common to island holidays: go to the top of the volcano / mountain, visit
the botanical gardens, shop at the ethnic market, drive out to some
remote fishing villages and check out the capital city. Decisions were easy
with a week's worth of doings and then home. I liked the driving too – it
seemed a symbol of the happy directionlessness of the days away,
spinning along empty roads to nowhere in particular.

Vague Memory

The church was classical
we held hands, it was warm

tourists were elsewhere
the man was selling something

we bought whatever it was
because he was alone there

and he was old or maybe
it seemed cheap at the price

then he wanted his photo taken
and he laughed at having no teeth

for the picture that just fell from the shoebox
of the day we bought something

from an old man outside a church
somewhere on an island, once.

I imagine this pilgrimage will have a similar, if more energetic,
momentum. It's time out and away from normal life. There are fewer and
different decisions to take and most of them boil down to one of two –
what (to wear or carry) and when (to eat, drink or sleep). Rather than
drive around an island, all I have to do is put one foot in front of the other
for two hundred miles or so. The difference though is in motivation. Our
island holidays were for refreshment and we didn't embrace physical

hardship, seek atonement nor explicitly express gratitude. And we didn't attempt to bridge the gap between the living and the departed by deliberately venerating the relics of a saint. Whilst the pilgrimage has many holiday elements, the intention is also to consciously change the self and her view of the world. Or so I hope.

On that first day I carry too much and trust too little. Leaving León, I buy a picnic at a mini-market making my rucksack heavier and more awkward with a bobbing carrier bag of plums on top and bread rolls, cheese and a plastic bottle of water stuffed in an outside pocket.

Soon, I see that there are drinking fountains at regular intervals so there's no need to carry more than my easily re-filled little flask of water. The picnic too is redundant – at just about lunch time, after crossing a dismal industrial estate, I come to Virgén del Camino, a strip of shops and cafes along a busy road, where the smell of frying potatoes and tapas, and the sight of espresso in little white cups, glasses of cool beer and wedges of tortilla, remind me that I'm not in the wilderness at all, just a suburb of León where lunch can be easily had.

There are few other pilgrims on that first morning. A young woman in lycra, whom I will see again at the end of my walk, slows down to chat before she zips past me. She's Argentinian and walked the length of France before succumbing to huge blisters which mean she's been resting in Barcelona for some weeks before continuing. In her twenties, she has the glossiness of a rich person and is sleek as a gazelle. Her outline is slender as she skips over a footbridge and disappears ahead of me. Such speed and grace seem totally unattainable as I struggle to find a rhythm, to feel my way into my journey and breathe easily. Instead I walk awkwardly, alternately tightening and loosening the straps of my pack, with my bothersome plums in their rustling plastic bag bouncing round my ears.

Gratifyingly, on the hot open road through a deserted industrial estate, I overtake two women who move with the serenity of someone's pet cows. They look like Native Americans, are tall like giants and are carrying enormous packs. They lumber rather than walk and are smiling, talking peacefully. I puff and chuff my way past them and never see again. This to-ing and fro-ing will be a feature of the *camino*, like the ebb and flow of waves on a beach. People pop up unexpectedly time and again, or disappear forever leaving no chance of saying goodbye. I still have a pang thinking of the handsome Swede, the jolly man from Alsace and the sweet Italian girl that I loved and lost along the way.

I cross the main road to head out into the countryside. In the distance are rolling hills hazed by bright sunshine, inviting me west but, in the foreground, the sandy soil is churned up with tracks leading to what is evidently a new road system being built. It's a confusing, ugly picture. The path seems to veer off to the left but at the end of the concrete track, before it gives way to sand and rubble, there's a series of giant painted yellow arrows, pointing to the right. Some pilgrims pass me, merrily trotting in the direction suggested by the painted arrows. There are no other landmarks, no signposts anywhere, just the mess of construction and despoiled land.

I follow the old route to higher ground and once again, there are more dusty paths heading in different directions, a main road slicing the landscape and a village on the horizon to my left. It still makes no sense – it's a rerun of the morning's search for the office to get my *credencial*. I panic, thinking I'm lost again. Then in the hazy light I see what look like rucksacked pilgrims in profile on the horizon, heading up the bank to the main road, and carrying on in the opposite direction from the village. So I go that way and, as I get closer, see a bright blue and yellow sign with a stick-figure pilgrim, a scallop shell reduced to a fanned-out series of lines, and a clear arrow pointing the way along a stretch of new road. It's easy to know which way to go, blindingly obvious in fact. All I need to do is follow the painted arrows and forget any attempt at orienteering.

That first afternoon, I begin to learn a few lessons that as the days go on, become second nature. The first is that you can't get lost. Or at least, you have to be extraordinarily unobservant, to the point of contrariness, to even get the smallest bit lost. Over the years, particularly recently with EU funding, the Way has got more and more thoroughly sign-posted and documented so there are signs everywhere.

There's a whole ecology and economy of sign design, planning, man-ufacture, distribution, erection and maintenance along the *camino*, apparently run by the provincial authorities as on my own stretch of the route, signs in Castile and León differ from those in Galicia. The main symbol is, of course, the scallop shell, because scallops were brought back across Europe from Galicia. There are signs set in the pavement and on the sides of buildings made of shiny brass, in three dimensions, cast like coins. Others are flat, flush to the wall or the ground. There are signs on signposts, signs with the number of kilometres to go, signs sponsored by the EU at the beginning of villages, showing where there's accommodation and places to eat. There are signs sponsored by beer companies. And there are big signs on the main road with a stylised pilgrim, tall and thin carrying an elongated pack and a great star symbolising Compostela. When there are no manufactured signs, someone with a pot of yellow paint, has marked the way with yellow arrows, handily on the corners of buildings or along walls at bifurcations along a country path. Sometimes there are many arrows, unequivocally agreeing that, yes, it goes that way. The people with pots of yellow paint pots are like a supernatural presence – Brownies doing a good turn or house sprites who dust, iron and wash up during the night so that in the morning the house is spick and span. They predict where pilgrims might pause or feel confused and help out with an arrow before anyone knows it's needed.

I must qualify my statement that you really can't get lost. It's true if you pay attention to the path as you walk and simply watch where you are going. If you try to consult a guidebook and take directions mediated by someone else who may have done it years ago, and perhaps wasn't completely clear even then, you're likely to go astray. If you look outward, at reality, rather than at what you think you know, you can't get lost. If I'd known that before I married, I would have seen the signs, the many yellow arrows telling me unequivocally to go the other way. I wasn't looking and I got lost.

Marriage seems like a linear journey from the point of conjoining until the moment death does its parting trick. Like a pilgrimage, it begins with desire, an inner longing and inkling, which translates into preparation and then setting out on a journey. It may end literally with a kissing of relics, a reverencing of the mortal remains of a loved one. But, between the beginning and the end, it has more in common with the spiralling peregrinations of the Celtic Christians or the medieval Irish pilgrims who, rather than heading for Santiago or Jerusalem, simply set out wandering on foot or in little boats 'for the love of Christ'. They had no identifiable destination, or rather, they were undertaking their journeys to discover a destination within.

Once we set out on our marriage journey, there were no maps, not even a sign as we entered a village to say where the resting places, shops and bars could be found. The yellow arrows were deceptive, pointing each of us in different directions, or missing entirely, leaving us arguing on a street corner, each convinced we knew best which route to take.

I hoped before anything else, that both of us would want to follow the same path, at the same pace, in the same way. My observations of couples on the *camino* give concrete examples of how difficult that can be, when one partner is inevitably faster, hungrier or more sociable than the other. You and I certainly set out together and the point of departure was clearly marked by invitations, a ceremony and a party, but there was no way of knowing the ending until we both reached it. And perhaps one of us was always headed for Santiago, whilst the other's idea of pilgrimage was to end up in Jerusalem or Rome or Bardsey Island, or simply to wander, trusting to God. At times, I felt like St Brendan bobbing around on my raft, trusting to luck, with no idea where I was headed or what storms and sea monsters I might encounter.

On one of our exploratory holidays in Cornwall, before we embarked on the voyage towards marriage, we visited St Wenna's Holy Well, now located in the bar of a hotel in the little village of St Wenn. Beneath the church tower, a punning sundial quotes Mark's gospel, reminding visitors, 'Ye know not when'. It was early days and we were head-over-heels in love and couldn't get enough of each other's company. Cornwall was a new and strange country to me and, of course, I was many years younger. Yes, I knew not Wenn. It's also true that now I know not how, nor why and even the 'what' is probably a post hoc rationalisation. And the what I think I know about us, what I'm writing here, is probably quite different from yours.

At last. I've cleared the suburbs of León. It's yet another beginning when the path turns off the hot road into a quiet hamlet with a school, a telephone box and a picnic table at which I sit and gnaw on crusty bread and replenish my water bottle. It's hot and hard to get going again after the route march through León. But soon, the *camino* becomes as I'd imagined – the path, a wide swathe of sandy red earth undulating through scrubby land, mostly dry and uncultivated but every so often yielding flashes of colour. There are wild blue crocuses with pointy petals sticking up in a ditch and dull grey grasshoppers suddenly transforming themselves in turquoise butterflies, taking off up and over the path as I walk. Other butterflies, buttercup yellow, fly past, in pairs, their dancing motion in contrast to my own plodding steps.

The morning was bright and cool, now it's getting steadily hotter as I walk for a few hours seeing no one else at all along the track, no houses nor signs of life, apart from the insects and occasional bits of toilet paper and wet wipes left in the thorny ditches either side.

The first settlement I come to looks like a Mexican village in a old Western. Wide streets cast long shadows from mud buildings and there's a hush that's either siesta or the silence of people who never leave their houses. The yellow arrows and scallop shells point walkers away from the village centre but another arrow suggests a detour to a café. The place is lively and noisy, packed with with locals and pilgrims. I have a double Fanta – the kind of drink that would usually be unpalatable but now, after the long, hot walk, is nectar, solid with sugar, icy cold, filling my mouth with zing and chemicals.

The cafe operates an informal apartheid with elderly Spanish gentlemen filling the bar, playing cards at little tables in what looks like a whist drive, sitting up straight in their shabby, formal clothes. Outside, a straggle of pilgrims, sweaty and dusty, sprawls with cold drinks on the shady veranda, feet up on the spare chairs. The rucksacks strewn around look like colourful turtles with straps and loops instead of legs.

Fortified, I set off for the final couple of miles along a lane. After walking alone all afternoon, I join other pilgrims bunching up and sepa-rating as the day draws to a close. I walk with Geoffrey, a Franciscan monk, originally from South Africa, now living in the Netherlands. We argue, politely, about the changes in South Africa. I'm unhappy with his claim that things are generally worse than before, under apartheid. My impressions from a working visit the year before and from my South African brother-in-law and his cousins, are that however difficult and uncertain the new country is, it has to be better than a repressive police state. Even pensioners I knew living in poverty in the chaotic new Russia after the collapse of the Soviet Union, told me said it was preferable to being in constant fear of arrest or imprisonment. Inevitably, I apply the same lens to our marriage and subsequent separation and divorce, convinced that repressive regimes are worse than the chaos that comes with new growth. Geoffrey though is equally sure of the opposite. Different lenses, different days, different people, different histories and we eventually agree, it's impossible to generalise and how can anyone know what will turn out to be better or worse?

I do know I'm tired and elated at the end of my first day. That Villar de Mazarife is surprising with its mud houses and over-sized storks' nests precarious on the tall belfries, that I have no idea what to expect from a hostel and don't know that tonight's is one of the more eccentric I will encounter on the way.

It reminds me more than anything of the sort of hippy hotels that now hardly exist in cities like Istanbul and Marrakech, like the one where Kate Winslett stays in the film of 'Hideous Kinky'. From the outside, it looks like a farm with enclosures of dry tussocky grass. The walls are covered with lurid murals on religious themes and also lots of graffiti, full of platitudes and messages of love. Two storeys of verandas open onto a central courtyard. There are small dormitories and then along the verandas, mattresses laid out side by side with no space between them. In spite of Geoffrey's warnings about mosquitoes, I opt to sleep outside.

Walking around the little town takes two minutes. There's another hostel with a horse tied up outside, a bar and more churches and storks' nests. It's quiet, closed-in, reminiscent of the Marquez stories where no one writes to the Colonel and eventually someone will come along and offer to take me to see ice.

In the bar, El Torre, I order a 'fish platter' at seven o'clock and it arrives at nine. Everything on the plate is orange with synthetic breadcrumbs and shiny with fat. Deep-fried squid, deep-fried prawns, deep -fried fish fingers, served with a 'Russian salad' of gloopy mayonnaise, flavourless iceberg lettuce topped with bright pink diced ham. It is so unlike the olive oil-drenched, spicy Spanish dish I'd anticipated, I want to laugh and cry.

It reminds me of a day in 2002, when you and I were in Moscow en route to Yasnaya Polyana. We hadn't been there for several years and many things had changed in the new 'new Russia'. In the old 'new Russia', taxis had disappeared but it was possible to zip around Moscow cheaply and interestingly in private cars, by hitch-hiking. Just move to the edge of the pavement, stick out a hand and within seconds, a car would screech to a halt and you negotiated a fare to wherever you wanted to go. You would then, usually, enjoy a pleasant conversation with an out-of-work musician or a scientist who was supplementing a meagre salary by giving lifts. We did this often on our early visits, researching the life of

Solzhenitsyn for your biography published in the late 1990s. I would sit in the front, telling the driver in execrable Russian what we were doing and where we going and you would ride in the back, reciting Pushkin like a madman to the delight of the driver.

By 2002 though, that system had disappeared and outside our hotel was an official taxi rank of white-sprayed Volgas, guarded by a line of thugs in expensive leather jackets – a million miles from the doe-eyed musicians or the scientists in shiny suits and pebble thick glasses who were the human side of an often hostile city. It was a sweltering summer's day, when we emerged hungry and looking for lunch from the Tretyakov Gallery, where we made a regular pilgrimage on all our visits to Moscow, and tried to 'flag down' a car. Motorists sailed by, bemused at this now outmoded behaviour. So we walked through the hot city, along the pretty boulevards of Zamoskvorechye, pollen from the plane trees floating around us. We were happy being in the country we both loved.

Eventually we found a restaurant in a leafy side street with tables outside. It was dreamy – the kind of romantic Russia depicted in the Mikhailkov film 'Burned by the Sun', alongside the never far away terror. We looked at the small menu which was another departure from the acres and acres of promised dishes which, as in Greece, the old Soviet-style restaurants promised but never delivered. And we chose the exotic sounding fish dish and wine and vodka and black bread. We were usually happiest when we'd been interestingly out and about and then sat in restaurants, having ordered, waiting for the food, you, in the old days smoking happily and both of us sipping our drinks. Being outside in old Moscow on a sunny day, waiting for what we imagined was perch or sturgeon, was blissful. And then, the fish fingers arrived, but not any old fish fingers, but truly lurid orange fish fingers, four each and an anaemic boiled potato and a pickle. And we laughed and didn't mind.

And here I was in Villar de Mazarife, a dusty village not very far west of León and the flat badlands of Northern Spain, surprised again by bright orange fish fingers, a plate shiny with the remains of deep frying and I'm not with you. And I'm not with you now as I write this and, possibly, will never be with you to tell you about it. How I was promised the sexy, salty taste of fish, its subtle whites and silvers and how the reality was chemical bread crumbs and the colour orange which in food belongs only to oranges.

The hostel is quietening down for the night. Two boys strum guitars downstairs, quite badly, and stumble through half-known lyrics in non-native English. It's a soothing lullaby. I snuggle into my sleeping bag. It's another moment of arrival, using it for the first time. Getting into bed at the end of a long day, combined with clean pyjamas and pillow case is doubly delicious. I supplement the sleeping bag with a couple of blankets and feel held and snug. It's an unexpected treat to sleep outside. I can see a rectangle of stars framed by the open courtyard and recognise Orion and the Plough and once again regret my lack of knowledge of any other constellations.

One of the possible origins of the word 'Compostela' is that it derives from the Latin *Campus Stellae*, meaning field of stars. Another, less romantic, etymology could be *Composita Tella* meaning burial ground. Somehow the two don't seem incompatible. Lying in the chilling, fresh air, well away from other sleepers I feel I could happily die. For me, it's a good litmus test of whether one is in the right place or not. I wouldn't want to die sitting around in a pub or watching TV but here, where my body aches pleasurably from the walk, is clean from the shower and still hungry from the only-just-touched orange extravaganza at the Torre, I feel as if my life is being well-used and paradoxically, so alive it wouldn't be at all bad to die. And I'm a whole 14.4 miles closer to Compostela.

Chapter Two

Alone again, naturally

Mazarife to Astorga, 27th September

When I wake in the half-light, I see people like shadows moving towards the showers and toilets or rolling up their sleeping bags. Others are applying plasters to their feet or just examining them with a kind of ritualistic wonder, sitting on the ground, bent over like Indian cobblers busy at their craft. I creep out to collect my laundry and the sky makes me gasp. The last time I saw such a sky was when I lived for six months after our divorce on a farm high on Bodmin Moor, with no other human habitation in sight. The Milky Way is another name for the Camino de Santiago and it always induces a sense of awe but here, it's especially surprising, seeing it so close to dawn. There are the countable, clearly identifiable stars and beyond them, a sprinkle of glitter, like damp crystals of salt on black velvet, the stardust that disappears, usually unobserverved, day after eternal day.

I set off soon after seven and walk from the perimeter of the village out into the dark along a straight road. Walk, walk, walk, walk – at last I've found a pleasing rhythm and every so often catch up and pass other pilgrims who loom suddenly in the darkness. My heart goes out to those hobbling along painfully with sticks and I wonder how far they've come. A popular starting point is St-Jean-Pied-de-Port, on the French side of the Pyrenees, where many routes from across Europe converge to form the Camino Frances, the French Way, into Spain. For those starting there, this would be their second or third week of walking. It's only my second day, no wonder I feel fresh in comparison.

I'm haunted by my friend Simon who died suddenly a few years ago. He had a great influence on my religious life and our friendship went through many different phases after our first meeting as lecturers at the same college in our early twenties. He came into a dream I had about the ancient theatre at Ephesus, which we visited together and just sat there watching me. It was the first time I'd had the sensation of someone 'coming to you in a dream' which feels very different from just dreaming 'about' someone. I wished he'd spoken in the dream, instead of just sitting, smiling knowingly, and told me what he wanted or why he was there. At Truro Cathedral this Easter, during the three hour Good Friday devotion, I was strongly aware of his presence behind me, in the place where we'd sat at a service together a decade before. I turned round several times, convinced I would see his familiar face. Like me, Simon was prone to periods of sloth and indecision and often failed to 'get on with it', that is, to become the much-loved Unitarian Minister he was when he died, until relatively late in life. And then, at the age I am now, he collapsed in the wine department of Tesco near Chester, his trolley full of tins of sardines and good quality red, and never regained consciousness.

My parents called me Mañana as a child and it can take me a long time to get round to things. And sometimes, I do nothing at all, very slowly. In spite of an instant connection, it took me a while to fall in love with you and then to break away. It didn't take long to marry you once I came to Cornwall but I probably should have left you sooner. One day, a few months before our wedding, I nearly did. An inner voice was telling me clearly to go and on a rare occasion when you were out of the house, I decided to act on it. You were giving a presentation at Torquay Grammar School which meant a long day away from Truro. Now though, I wonder whether, in fact, you were there at all and whether it was more likely some romantic assignation. A decade on, I marvel at my innocence. Of course, Torquay Grammar School is extremely unlikely to invite you to read. How plausible those lies were – and how numerous. But also how wonderful, my willingness to believe. Perhaps my gullibility was like a red rag to the story-making bull you are. As with any talent, it would be a shame not to exercise your ability to fictionalise, to show it off, to see just how far you can go.

It was a bright summer's day in 1999. I was letting out my house in London to friends and most of my stuff was still there. I'd brought with me to Cornwall only what would fit into my old white Ford Escort. I'd be able to move back to Charlton easily enough. That inner voice was insistent, 'Go, go, go!' and I ran round the house, filling my car with a studentish selection of books, clothes, favourite pots and pans and set off. I can't remember now where our dog Tamsin was – perhaps I thought she'd be okay for those few hours until you returned. I drove up the A30 with a rising sense of elation. In Cornwall, I often have a sense of both claustrophobia and precariousness, as if we could all be swept off that narrow granite ridge surrounded on all sides by sea, whether tranquil creeks or surf pounding against high cliffs, depending on the angle of any particular bit of coast. Everything narrows to Lands End, beyond which is the scatter of the Scilly Isles, then nothing but treacherous rocks and the Atlantic. Driving East gives a sensation of the land mass spreading, the sky getting bigger and the possibility of more roads at every junction, roads that fan out in all directions unlike those in Cornwall which are hemmed in by the coastline. Oh, it was good to feel the miles of the A30 being left behind as my car spun along. Crossing Goss Moor, before the dualling, was slow and then after a fast stretch, the road winds up onto Bodmin Moor with its gloomy hills and bright green lowlands dotted with sheep and wild ponies. Then it loops past Jamaica Inn and climbs steadily onto the high moorland. I was flying.

Suddenly, I pictured you returning from the station in a taxi, calling as you opened the door, 'Honey, I'm home.' – a line you quoted from the 1998 film 'Pleasantville', which we'd both found hilarious and thought-provoking. 'Honey, I'm home,' comes from earlier American TV sitcoms and is spoken more sinisterly by Jack Nicholson in Stanley Kubrick's film 'The Shining'. You, though, would call it out affectionately, 'Hi, honey, I'm hooome!'. And, probably only after you'd wandered into the kitchen, plonked yourself at the old farmhouse table with a bottle of red wine and an ashtray and spent a few minutes staring into the middle distance, would it dawn on you that the house was looking a little emptier and, oh, my car wasn't there and, yes, a few books and saucepans seemed to have disappeared. There's a scene in 'Pleasantville':

George: I came home like I always do. And I came in the front door. And I took off my coat. And I put down my briefcase and I said "Honey. I'm home."

[*The men all nod in recognition.*]

George: … Only no one was there. So I went into the kitchen and I yelled it again. "Honey – I'm home." But there was no one there either. No wife. No lights. No dinner.

[*The men all gasp*]

George: So I went to the oven you know – because I thought maybe she had made me one of those "TV dinner…" But she hadn't. She was gone. And I looked and looked and looked – but she was gone.

It seemed too sad. Back then, neither of us had mobile phones so there was no way I could call to tell you some story about being unexpectedly out and about. And there was no way of you calling me. The thought of you home alone was too poignant for me to bear. So, at the isolated little petrol station on the windy open road, near Dozmary Pool where King Arthur may have rowed out to receive Excalibur from the Lady of the Lake, I pulled in, turned the car around and hurtled back to Truro.

I finished putting my things back again just a few minutes before you returned, so it was me sitting at the kitchen table, red wine in one hand, Silk Cut in the other as you opened the door, 'Honey, I'm home!'. 'Pleasantville' is the Garden of Eden, a 1950s utopia with no sex or violence, to which two teenagers of the MTV generation find themselves magically transported. In 'Pleasantville' there are no roads out of town; Main Street simply carries on then goes round in a circle but the inhabitants don't notice. It was the same trying to leave you or Cornwall, somehow I was back where I started, although it was never Eden and now, honey, I'm no longer at home.

Perhaps if I'd crossed the Tamar Bridge, with its empty air in all directions and tiny boats beneath, it would have marked a transition and sheer momentum might have taken me all the way to London and a different life. I wouldn't still be in Cornwall ten years later feeling claustrophobic and restless but may well have been just as restless elsewhere, wondering why on earth I didn't stay with you.

Once in that pre-marriage period I found a letter you'd written to yourself asking whether it was wise for us to marry and wondering whether you wouldn't be better off with an older woman with decent foundation garments. I chose to ignore it – as I chose to ignore many things that were prescient or crazy. From my vantage point in the future, I want to shout at you, in answer to your introspections, 'No, don't marry me' and, 'Yes! Find an older woman'. And yet you've done it again, married someone even younger than me who is as likely to be mistaken for your grandaughter as your daughter.

On the *camino*, it would be truly crazy to run forward, then hurry back and then stop for ten years. It's clearly a forward motion along a specific path and even if it slows down, it never entirely stops. One of the universal rules of the *albergues* that pilgrims can stay for just one night and they must then move on. Moving on isn't an option, it is the whole *raison d'etre*.

Walking in the pre-dawn dark is thrilling and a sense of the unknown compensates for the dull topography. I can see very little, just the outline of a long straight road heading towards the black shadow of the hills beyond. I must be heading due west as dawn is breaking behind me. If I look ahead, everything's black and velvety, but if I turn round, it's as if a light has been switched on to reveal a pink, yellow and orange horizon with the sun blazing above it.

I arrive at the first hamlet, hungry and thirsty, daring to hope for breakfast. It's Sunday, everywhere's shuttered and deserted-looking but then, joy of joys, I spot a black cat in the window of a bar, a small sign of life, suggesting it might be open for business. Having walked quite a few miles that morning without breakfast, the hit from the double espresso and *pain au chocolat* is like electricity switching on the circuits of my brain and body. I leave the cafe turbo-charged and invincible.

I miss the rhythms of a household. In single life no one cares what you do, the days are saggy and unstructured, dinner might be muesli at midnight, legs stay unwaxed all winter and it's possible to read in bed with a bright light on all night if you want with no one to complain. Our home life had a predictable routine around which the days unfolded. It was your third marriage and you were already sixty four and a creature of habit. Once, I did your horoscope and discovered that as well as our shared Aquarian suns, your chart is full of elements concerned with the home, family, connections and routine. I especially liked the mornings, the most optimistic time of day for me, when I'd be up first, making myself tea and tidying in the early hours.

Early

The whole house is soft with sleep
the beloved sinks deep

beneath waves of feathers
the dog twitches, stretching

across the sofa and the cat curls
on her hidden head under the radiator

I spread gorse-coloured butter,
over bread which crumbles like night-thoughts

my body slow with tenderness
for these other-worldly beings, who though

touched by morning light, birdsong
wind, the faint roar of a waking world

stay far away, here but there, vaguely aware
of love, like breath, invading their dreams.

Tamsin, ultra-senstive to the sound of the faraway step of the paper boy,
at some point would begin barking maniacally. She'd run up and down
the stairs, getting ready to meet the newspaper as it was pushed through
the letter box of the upstairs porch. Every day, the same intruder. Not
long afterwards, there'd be the sound of you getting out of bed, peeing,
padding downstairs, making a pot of tea, no milk, two slices of toast with
jam or marmalade and carrying it all on a tray upstairs and back to bed,
where you'd read The Times for an hour, filling the bed with sharp
crumbs and tea stains, before taking a bath and walking along the
upstairs corridor to your desk. When The Times went tabloid, it was as if
the world had come off its axis, things weren't as they should be. For a
while you took The Telegraph, still broadsheet, not able to face The
Guardian where you'd had a love-hate relationship years before.
Eventually though, you went back to The Times, with The West Briton

on Thursdays and I added in The Guardian on Saturdays. The daily
newspaper was an anchor for you, so that even on holiday, finding a
paper was vital to ensuring the day started properly. During my first trip
to Cornwall soon after we met, I was surprised that you were so determined to find a copy of the The West Briton, the parochial local
newspaper. You told me that long after I left, The Guardian was still
delivered on Saturdays, perhaps it still is and the ghost of me is there at
the kitchen table reading it.

We'd do our own thing for the next few hours, me working on the arts-
education project which was one of the things that kept me in Cornwall.
If I hadn't found a job, I may well have left earlier but I was offered an
interesting year-long consultancy the same weekend in 1999 that I got
married, anchoring me two times over to this almost-island.

Then at eleven, coffee. If I was at home, I'd be working in the spare
room and later the shed I converted to an office. We'd email each other,
enjoying the novelty of the new medium, then meet at the battered
kitchen table. I was still intermittently smoking and would puff one of
your Marlboros or, if I was being cautious, my own Silk Cut. And we'd
look at each other across the table – that act of looking at you across a
table conjures a thousand memories of different conversations and
different tables around the world, your serious, handsome, loved face
and your dark eyes gazing into mine and seeing who knows what. Our
talk was never meaningless. It was sometimes difficult and too often me
complaining and you denying but there was so much to say and so much
still unsaid that now at eleven I miss that ritual, that habit, that bit of the
marriage pattern. Jackie Kay's poem 'Mugs' describes how she and her
soon-to-be ex still kept to the ritual of making each other a cup of tea,
even though both knew that a split was imminent and I understand the
impulse. You are inscrutable in many ways and never said much about
your feelings for me after we married, but in 2006, you sent me the
following poem after I'd called in one day. It describes one of those small
'spots of time' that Wordsworth talks of in the Prelude. Every day, there's
an eleven o'clock that for some years was a spot of time with you, me, a
cafetière, a packet of cigarettes, a jug of milk and an ashtray, sometimes
in the company of others, more usually just the two of us, you looking
out over the gravelled area between the house and hedge, me looking
inwards to the kitchen, each of us looking into each other's eyes and

talking about this and that. Like the bottle of wine being opened at six and the daily preparing of the vegetables, these are the holy offices of domestic life and days are empty without them.

Morning Coffee

It's become very proper, as it never was,
Not even in our first moment of shaking hands.
We cannot say, 'Our marriage failed because…'

I re-fill your mug, and am awkward at a pause
In our chat about no longer mutual friends;
It's become very proper, as it never was

When, here, we sipped each other, separate straws
In the rich drink that changes as it stands.
We cannot say, 'Our marriage failed because

Of this betrayal, or those quirks and flaws';
It passed as slowly as this Fall descends.
It's become very proper, as it never was.

'Oh, well, why not?' – you pluck a Marlboro as
You did when fingers tingled. Where guilt lands
Neither can say: only, It failed because.

Our half-blind cairn still slowly moves its paws
Across the stones to greet you. No love ends,
But now it's proper, as it never was,

Just kissing cheeks on parting. Sadness gnaws
Alongside gratitude that we are friends.
The mystery of love; there never was
A time we could explain it with 'because…'

Revived by the inky Spanish coffee with its spoonful of sugar, I'm impatient to embrace the sunny Sunday in Spain and join the other pilgrims on the Way ahead. As I come out of the cafe, I hear loud singing in French. A man of around sixty, tanned, smiling, dressed in spruce navy, knotty brown legs in shorts and boots, and a knotty staff to walk with, is greeting passing pilgrims with songs. One couple hurries on by, looking embarrassed, and he reprimands them in French, saying that the *camino* is about Joy not Misery. They look even more uncomfortable and walk faster and he responds by mimicking them, their dogged, head-down gloomy way of walking.

For the next little while, there's a wide track with pilgrims all heading their one way at different speeds, catching up, dropping back, like cars and lorries on a motorway. I fall into conversation with the Frenchman, who apparently comes from the Auvergne and walks the *camino* regularly. I'm surprised my French comes back so easily and enjoy telling him about 'Cornouaille' and its connection with the *camino*. We flirt, I think, but perhaps that's his way with everyone, a mixture of openness, song and sweetness. I dub him 'Monsieur La Joie' and he, watching me speeding along, calls me, 'Madame TGV' (the *Train Grande Vitesse.*). This small attentiveness pleases me – a nickname feels personal and special. You never used nicknames but called me darling, less often after we married and then Victoria, Victoria, Victoria. I liked my full, pompous, over-syllabled name when I heard it pronounced aloud by you.

The road crosses a roundabout into Órbigo, one of the historic towns on the route. An eighteenth century stone bridge stretches across the river and is its main tourist attraction. The town is pretty with hanging baskets and tidy streets. It's clearly a popular destination for coach parties – something I would see more of towards the end of the pilgrimage. The tourists are in Sunday mood, mostly placid, plump Spaniards leaning over the historic bridge, photographing each other, taking their time, unlike the rest of us in boots and backpacks who, even as we pause, have half an eye on the time and the need to press on. I sit for a while on a bench and write some postcards, feeling dreamy and rootless in this little town. A drinking fountain bubbles under some plane trees and I have a sense of being nowhere in particular – well into this journey yet out of time and far from my usual commitments and connections. In just over a day, the *camino* has become my life. I feel several stages in now – the plane, the train, the first day's walking done, the being lost, the staying in a hostel – as if doing everything once is enough for it to become familiar and normal

I buy some bread and a few apricots in a little grocers, one of the few shops open, and carry on, meandering onto wide tracks like those that criss-cross the South Downs. The weather gets hotter and there's little shade from the scrubby oaks. Pilgrims are fewer and more dispersed.

Every so often, I pass a depressing heap of litter, then a farm, then a group of elderly peasants, picking grapes in the throbbing heat, their heads covered by headscarves or trilbies. The path curves and climbs, and on I plod until eventually I see, a long way in the distance, a huge cross on a ridge. It's encouraging to have something to aim for and then, wonderful, once I've eventually crested the ridge, to look down on the city of Astorga with its magnificent cathedral shimmering on the plain below. A man is selling cake, pop and water from a trolley, black and alive with flies. He must have dragged everything a long way up from the valley below and sadly no one is buying.

The litter bothers me. I want to pick it up but there's too much. At least I'd like to know who might. The path is only a line through the landscape so the land around it is presumably owned or controlled by someone. The phrase, 'Whose woods these are I think I know' comes to mind as I muse on whose fields these might be. Your love of Robert Frost is a legacy I've inherited from our marriage. And right behind Robert Frost, there trots in Housman and his 'blue remembered hills'. And with each of them a flood of memories of a weekend in Shropshire driving along Wenlock Edge and you buying me a collection of Housman's poems. We stayed in a romantic hotel where the only drawback was communal breakfasts round a large table. We were sulky and naughty, still making love all night, until we were drunk and stunned with it the next day and incapable of small talk over the scrambled eggs.

We'd sit in the hotel's conservatory and you'd critique my attempts at writing poetry. Shropshire astonished me with its emptiness, the bare expanses of Long Mynd and the heart-breaking ruined abbey at Much Wenlock. Only on walking the *camino* have I started feeling as well as knowing about the tragedy and vandalism of the 'dissolution of the monasteries'. The word 'dissolution' sounds so neutral, something dissolving painlessly into something else, like the powdered hangover cures of our early relationship disappearing into a glass of water. In fact it was the loss of a heritage, a mindset and a way of ordering the world that can't be regained. And yet, like Henry, I was willing to dissolve something important, our marriage, our love, our book-knitted home, in the interests of moving on, rationality and something better. Appropriately, those hangover cures were called 'Resolve'. I resolve to remember all the books you've ever given me, as much a record of our relationship as holiday snaps or family milestones.

You often found it easier to use someone else's words and were a master at quoting from poetry, Shakespeare and other sources. It was a party game you excelled at, although your daughter stymied you once by asking for a quotation about shopping. You first gave me books when we met on the island of Skyros, a pile of your own, brought with you to sell on to students. I'd just finished a three and a half year posting in Moscow and we'd already agreed I would accompany you on your next research trip to Russia. You inscribed the books with quotations from Pushkin: 'I thought you had forgotten, heart!,' scribbles, kisses, explosive 'I love you!'s and comments like 'Tomorrow I shall be bereft – but MOCKBA!', 'Je t'aime' 'Я тебя люблю'. I hunt out my Robert Frost – a Penguin edition you gave me in November 96. That was over a year after we'd met but before we married. You were still passionate and playful, but the inscriptions are already less crazy than a year before. The book is full of your annotations and highlighted favourite poems. At the front, you've written a key: '√ = I like √√ = I love' and further down, 'For Victoria √√'. And you've included a poem in your own hand that you quoted to me often – 'Never again would birdsong be the same / And to do that to birds was why she came'. It was written by Frost for his secretary who later became his wife in a happy second marriage.

That expressiveness died when we married and I wonder where it went, whether I killed it or whether married life in your old home, guilt, legitimacy, my own ambivalence were to blame, diluting the intoxicating liquor that was our love affair. And yet the witnesses remain, those many books lined up on my shelves, paperbacks of poetry, catalogues you bought in the shops of museums and galleries we visited, second-hand books from wanderings in North America, all dated, annotated, gifts of your heart. I look too for Housman – I know he's here somewhere as I'd missed the book and asked you for it fairly recently – the process of separating our libraries was as incomplete as our separation from each other – but it's gone astray and the rising panic I feel is only partly to do with not being able to find a book. I want to record that there was a time when you'd buy me paperbacks of poetry and write at the front 'Victoria √√'.

The cathedral in Astorga looks close from the hill-top but the approach takes forever. Some malevolent joker seems to get pleasure from sending pilgrims away from the city that's so clearly straight ahead, via main roads going the other way and tracks that painstakingly circumnavigate dusty maize fields behind factories. There's yet another detour, when I think I've finally reached the city limits, of climbing a high footbridge over the electricity cables alongside the railway. There are half a dozen metal staircases that zigzag vertiginously up and then down again the other side, a hard climb at the end of hot day. Then, the way veers left instead of right round the ring road until, finally, there's a long cobbled ascent up into the old walled city.

The Santa Siervas de María Hostel is the first *albergue* in the town, not counting a miserable-looking house on a boggy triangle of land between the ring road and the railway, where the owner begs me to stay, promising showers, breakfasts, beds. Being out of season means there are no worries about finding beds, the hostels are unlikely to be full. Santa Siervas is brand new and gleaming but occupies an ancient mellow building. Completely different from the Middle-Eastern hippy-style hostel of last night, this is like a wholesome Scandinavian youth hostel, everything spick and span, with bossy, friendly signs everywhere and clean rooms of just four beds in two bunks.

On the bunk above me is an Italian woman in her early twenties. She's slender with shiny long dark hair and her eyes are wide with sadness. I learn that Roberta's unhappy after seeing her ex-boyfriend on Facebook, enjoying himself with a new girlfriend, and, what's more, the skin on her legs is dry in this heat. I'm able to help with the latter, giving her a tiny bottle of body lotion pilfered from a hotel somewhere. She's walking alone and has come all the way from France to mend a broken heart. She's truly lovely and I want to kill the boyfriend, or at least challenge him to a duel and shout, 'Allez, commence' and leave him scarred by swords and salt. My Italian is meagre so I'm not able to say so, but we compare hamstring and quadriceps stretching exercises before I head into town.

I've never heard of Astorga and its gorgeousness. The town is glitzy and this evening is busy with Spaniards on their *paseo* in the comfortable warm dusk. The square is full of multi-generational families, children running up and down, parents reprimanding them and grandparents sitting back in their cafe chairs, gazing contentedly around. The shops are the kind of impractical ones you get in tourist towns – selling souvenirs or luxury food. There are dozens of pastry shops and artisan chocolate shops with opulent windows, run by elderly women with firmly set hair, wearing floral frocks and thick stockings.

This evening my emotions run away with me, as if I am riding a horse I can't control. I want to be with people, I want to be by myself. I love seeing the Spanish bourgeoisie enjoying their Sunday recreation yet feel full of class rancour. I want to eat a good meal but I'm not hungry. I want to chat with someone and I want to be alone with my thoughts. I'm finding it hard even to be with myself. 'Bugger off, go away,' I say to this pain-in-the-arse 'me' who is following me around. 'No, you go, you bugger off,' she replies, 'I was here first.'.

This is the light and shade of being, and the difficulty of intimacy. When I'm sunny, you're night-time, when I'm sad and raining, you're irritated, looking for a brisk wind or a storm to break the atmosphere. How do couples do it? Or what is the cost to the one lucky enough to be riding a steady, unblinking horse, whilst his or her partner tags along, their own mount yanking at the bit, bending down to eat grass or prancing in a frenzy?

In the end, I sit with my diary in a cafe watching other people, spotting pilgrims. I see a pair of attractive Dutchmen, smoking little cigarillos, reading their guidebooks to the *camino*. They're drinking sherry and look serene and sophisticated. I'd like to talk to them but they're in their own male world of aromatic tobacco, slumped down on their seats in a way they wouldn't be with a woman alongside. Another pair of men, Spaniards, sit next to me. Ten years previously, I'm sure someone would have moved to chat me up, offer to buy me a drink or at least make eye contact. I feel that I am still the same as I was at twenty, nubile, attractive but the world tells me something different, that I'm gradually becoming invisible, like most middle-aged women. In some ways, it's comfortable, not being bothered, but perhaps eventually, I'll want to dye my hair, think harder about how I look – otherwise, as someone recently said to me, we might as well all be dressed in orange boiler suits, Guantanamo-Bay style.

The noise level from the local families ratchets up a few notches and as night falls, the restaurants begin to get ready for dinner. Time to go. A final wander around the magnificent city centre with its grandeur and Gaudi palace and back to the *albergue*. I check my laundry among the miles of lines at the back of the building and find it's already dry in the steady evening heat. Passing the kitchen, I see Roberta and a young man sitting at a table – he's playing with her long silky hair. I'm envious – of both of them – and at the same time relieved it's not me sitting there wondering what will happen next.

Chapter Three

Hobgoblin nor foul fiend

Who would true valour see, Let him come hither:
One here will constant be, come wind, come weather.
There's no discouragement shall make him once relent
his first avooowed intent to to be a pilgrim.

John Bunyan joins me today and won't leave, burrows into my brain like a mind-worm and spins his way through all the nooks and crannies, forcing me to sing. He wrote those words in 1684 whilst serving twelve years in Bedford Gaol for preaching without a licence. The poem was tidied up by Percy Dearmer and set to Monks Gate, an English folk tune, by Vaughan Williams. Percy Dearmer's version is better-known but I like Bunyan's original reference to foul fiends and hobgoblins. As someone commented, the 'quaint sincerity of the words stirs us out of our easy-going dull Christianity to the thrill of great adventure.'

And my time with you could be described as a great adventure – a word that has walked its way through Old French for chance, fortune and luck, via Latin for 'a thing about to happen', and, then, in Middle English acquiring elements of risk and danger. In the early fourteenth century, it became a 'perilous undertaking' before morphing in into a 'novel or exciting incident' and re-acquiring its letter – *d* –. In Cornwall recently, I met a writer, your age, the mother of a friend, who moves in the literary circles of North London. She was astonished to find out I'd been married to you. She knew of you during your most famous years, when you were linked with an eminent woman novelist of her acquaintance and scandal was breaking in the national press. Those times have a mythological quality for me. I was in my late teens then and a village girl for whom 'writers' might as well have been living on another planet.

This mother-of-a-friend looked me deep in the eyes and asked, 'My dear, did you suffer?'. The question bugged me – and one answer is, 'Yes, I did'. I was at times confused, humiliated, cross, sad and puzzled but never felt I didn't have choices. Now, with the years passing and with every step I take towards Santiago de Compostela, I see my time with you as a real adventure with its mixture of chance, fortune, luck, risk and peril.

It's not just Christianity that can seem dull, the world in general has lost much of its strangeness and it seems, as John Berger wrote, that there's no longer 'an elsewhere'. It's partly the need for an elsewhere which drew me to the *camino*. It's not a particularly perilous undertaking, and Spain's no longer very foreign and communication is, these days, instant. But the activity itself – going on a pilgrimage in our late capitalist, secular, consumer culture is a strange one. What Robert Macfarlane calls the 'nearby wild' and the 'bigness outside ourselves' had shrunk for me during the five years since we divorced. The 'nearby' here in Cornwall, and probably anywhere, is full of interest but became cosy through too much familiarity and I'd lost a sense of the bigness outside myself. It was not so much the external bigness to be found in foreign countries or wild scenery but the internal bigness of the risky and challenging landscapes of intimacy. You were as exotic as the Rocky Mountains or Gobi Desert to me with all your complexity and presence. Five years on, in spite of absorbing work, good friends and travel abroad, I was bored on an existential level.

I tried to go on a pilgrimage a few years before this one to Santiago. The then Dean at Truro Cathedral told me many times how wonderful Lindisfarne, Holy Island, is and the idea of walking across a causeway at low tide, appealed. Lindisfarne is an island that's almost not-an-island. Cornwall on the other side of the country, which although attached to Britain, is an almost-island. I booked trains and a week's retreat and packed my rucksack and wellingtons. But I felt dreadful on the day I was due to travel. I managed to get on the Falmouth-Truro branch line and sank my throbbing head onto my rucksack, inwardly groaning and fearing I would throw up. It was Saturday morning and the train was full of teenagers going to Truro to shop or hang out. Six boys behind me were loudly joshing and bantering, shouting and matily punching each other. One noticed me drooping over my rucksack, eyes closed. He leaned over the seat and shouted at the top of his voice, inches from my available ear – WAKE UP! before slipping quickly back into his own place so that when I wearily lifted my head, I'd no idea which boy had shouted. They all sat innocently staring into the middle distance, whistling or pretending to admire the passing countryside, chests heaving with barely supressed laughter. And so it continued for the half hour to Truro. Me, dropping my head, which felt as if it contained a steel works, a tannery and a Grand Prix race, all at full pelt, and then, at random intervals, an adolescent male voice, so close I could feel his intake of breath, yelling, WAKE UP! Every time, I'd lift my head like a wary tortoise and look at them pitifully, until eventually the boys, still managing to avert their gaze, were convulsed with mirth, their long legs and big feet lifting and jerking all over the place, tears pouring down their faces. In Truro, I staggered over the platform and onto the London train but was sick near Bodmin Parkway and abandoned the trip to go home and nurse a migraine in the comfort of my own bed. But, in spite of my misery at the time, I saw the joke and still think those boys were funny and also, wise. That injunction WAKE UP! is one I wish I'd heard more often and earlier in my life. The six of them, gawky in their too-tight white t-shirts, seem like a band of angels, reminding me that living life half-asleep, is at best, a waste of time. Setting out to Santiago was following a call to wake up.

Margery Kempe is a vivid example of a woman who hopes to find herself and get closer to God by going on pilgrimages to 'divers places of religion'. She seems to have had psychotic episodes after childbirth and when she recovers, has unsuccessful attempts at running a brewery and then a millers before heeding calls to become sexually chaste and give up eating meat. She eventually leaves her husband and fourteen children and takes off on constant pilgrimage, a true adventurer.

An even earlier woman pilgrim, Egeria, who was probably a Spanish nun and may have come from Galicia, made her way to Jerusalem somewhere around 381 to 384 AD, only fifty years after the reign of Constantine. Egeria comes across as a gentle person, systematically and diligently recording her visits to holy sites, in such a way that her 'Travels' can still be used as a guidebook today. Egeria is polite and grateful, self-effacing and always interested to meet holy men. 'who so willingly welcomed so unimportant a person as me to their cells'. Unlike, Margery, Egeria doesn't have a strong sense of entitlement.

I'm experiencing the *camino* as a way of walking into a bigness, where I can exist alongside the bits of me that are, for better or worse, Margery and Egeria. The *camino* has an historical and cultural bigness that is based on more than a series of old buildings and towns along a particular route but incorporates the whole of European history, the events of centuries past and also the individual beliefs and experiences of everyone who's ever encountered the *camino* and changed it in some small way, simply by being there. The bigness is permeable, like an invisible net, it encompasses mystery well beyond time and place, such as pilgrimages in Japan or the impulse that led to cave paintings and rituals faraway in, say, the South Seas.

That sense of an inner and outer vastness is enhanced by the silence of walking. I find it easier to be deeply quiet when walking than when sitting cross-legged to meditate. There's a paradox that by acknowledging what I'm passing, by noticing beauty, registering other people, getting feedback from various achy bits of my body, my interior world is more able to empty itself. The emptying is a process, like the way the water of a stream constantly passes, rather than a state, like an empty room. By walking in silence, letting the world pass through me, my inner landscape becomes richer, less inhabited by 'myself' but open to various presences, which I feel as God in various forms. That is the 'bigness' that is full of love and adventure, that's a calling to valour and constancy. Walking doesn't guarantee such presences but it creates space for them and helps the littleness, the petty thoughts and resentments to dissipate. It's much harder to fight with giants, hob-goblins and foul fiends at 4am, tossing and turning on a hot pillow in a sleepless bed. Out here on the Way, God simply takes up more room, squeezing them out, and is harder to ignore.

The hostel in Astorga is almost oppressively clean and purposeful. Instead of the ghostly gettings-up of the day before, there's the sound of brisk showers, smell of shampoo, the efficient zipping up of rucksacks and a purposeful murmur of voices. I too, get up in a business-like fashion and am soon efficiently on the road. It's early in Astorga, still dark, shops are shuttered, a street-sweeping machine chunders by and there are the silhouettes of rucksacked pilgrims ahead of me. The streets, even devoid of local people, still give off their air of affluence and comfort. Although it's undeniably a beautiful city, I find it somehow complacent and learn later that the Roman city was built on a Celtic settlement. Perhaps that tension between the Romans' love of order and control and the looser, more informal structures of the Celts is what's bugging me.

Conventional marriage seems a more Roman affair, in the way it puts walls around love, then patrols them with centurions and creates structural hierarchies, bishoprics and formality. I long for the kind of love, whether human or for God, that has more in common with the Celtic way of doing things. I especially enjoy stories of the Cornish saints like St Nectan, carrying his own severed head back to his hermitage and re-attaching it, or those early holy men, standing neck-deep in cold water for the sheer love of Christ. As I move further from you in so many ways, I find myself drawn to that strange world of bygone Cornwall, the medievals and feel close to the early pilgrims in their filthy clothes with their sinfulness and merriment.

After the suburbs of Astorga, I carry on along pretty lanes as the day gets brighter and the pilgrims more numerous. The road gives way to tracks which are suddenly unaccountably busy – perhaps more people start their pilgrimages in Astorga than León. The Way here is more like a motorway of pedestrians, incredibly varied in their sizes and shapes, quantities of luggage and levels of fitness.

I walk again for a while with Monsieur La Joie and he carries on calling me Madame TGV. His joy is truly contagious and thinking about him months later will still bring a smile to my face. I wonder how he lives back in the Auvergne, whether he sings all day there too, whether he has a wife or family. Somehow it seems likely that he's single and solitary, channelling his joy straight from some mysterious life-spring and offering it to the world, like an ancient saint in a hermitage on the wild cliffs in Cornwall.

He stops or I drop back, or vice versa. In any case, we lose each other. We're like flotsam being carried downstream in a river where one twig sticks in the bank and another leafy branch gets carried forward, until it's caught in an eddy with other bits and bobs. Then the twig is suddenly released by the pressure of yet more water bound headlong to the sea and springs loose and catches up with the branch. Some pilgrims, for whatever reason, may stop their journey, become stuck between rocks like the cup Thomas Hardy and Emma Gifford lost on their picnic in the Valency Valley when it fell into the Jordan and disappeared.

I fall in with the two Dutchmen I'd watched smoking their cigarillos in Astorga. Only they aren't Dutch. Hamish is, unsurprisingly, Scottish, from Dunkeld, the home of a poet friend of mine, and Clive is English and both of them live in South London. It doesn't take long to discover that Clive's son, his partner and their new baby are in Penryn, just a few miles away from me in Falmouth. Both men are very tall. Clive, the more lithe, walks easily, he's doing the second half of the Camino having walked from St-Jean-Pied-de-Port to León the year before. Hamish is having difficulty finding a rhythm, he has new boots and puffs slightly. They're both using walking poles and are setting a cracking pace that's hard even for me, a TGV, to match. Their aim is to shave a day from the usual itinerary and get to Santiago extra quickly in order to make a certain plane home. That strikes me as a pity, to be so pressed for time on only their third day. Also, I like their company and feel sad that they're whizzing off ahead. I say goodbye and begin to feel it's time for breakfast.

Margery Kempe rarely mentions the practicalities of pilgrimage apart from who gives her money for the next stage and focuses almost entirely on her prayers, visions and devotions. Egeria doesn't say much about her personal spirituality but is diligent and precise when describing buildings, landscapes and the religious services she attends. Neither of them appears to record what, when or where they ate.

This particular pilgrim though, once she starts thinking about breakfast, can't focus on anything else. I stop at a picturesque hamlet called Santa Catalina. It has a resort feel to it and is geared up for the pilgrims in a way I haven't seen before with inviting cafes and shops selling walking paraphanelia. After no real fresh food for two days, it's bliss to have a fried egg and freshly squeezed orange juice and buy bread and a banana to take away. I sit in the sun, feeling fit, well, satisfied, totally in the moment, enjoying the spectacle and banter of people passing.

The hours between a late breakfast and a late lunch are the easiest physically. As the days pass, I discover that a crack-of-dawn coffee, sweet, oily and inky fuels me for the burst into the dawn when I'm still half dreaming and the other people unidentifiable shadows, houses still dark and dawn is yet to arrive as a seeping stain on the horizon behind me. The coffee's enough to over-ride the sleepiness and any stiffness or protest in my not-fully-awake body. Then, as the world moves into clarity and faces become more defined, hunger builds and breakfast around ten is perfect and, for someone with a puritanical streak, all the more appetising because it's been earned by a few hours of walking rather than just sleeping.

Then the walking becomes more trance-like and lovely. The confines of a path and a body walking along it, melt away and the world shows itself to be infinite and eternal. There's the presence of God and then angels start arriving. Some of the angels are human ones in the form of walking companions, bringing their various messages, either in conversation or simply the fact of their presence in the world. Others are the various angels of Gaia: butterflies and birds, flowers and trees, sunshine or rain. As the days pass, there seem to be more ghosts. I find myself thinking a lot about people I've known who've died. The euphemism 'passed over' makes sense on the *camino*, as if they've simply moved on more quickly or slowly than me and I've lost them along the Way, in the same way as I've lost those companions whose company I enjoyed but never see again. The presence though of the dead friends and relatives as I walk, thinking about them and remembering times we shared, becomes real. Even though I can't see them, I feel that they are close enough for me to sense their breath on my skin or pick up their scent on the breeze.

I reach Rabanal, the envisioned overnight stop, at midday, far too early to find a bed for the night. The path too is still inviting, beckoning me on like the famous mermaid of Zennor, in the far West of Cornwall, who sang on her rock, luring local boy Matthew Trewella over the cliff edge. Leaving pretty Rabanal, the track lifts itself from the plain like a ribbon with the wind beneath it, enticing me onwards. It's as if hands are assisting a carrier pigeon to take flight, to head for the haze of mountains. For two days, the mountains have been far off in the distance but now they are right in front of me, blue and looming, a mysterious mass of which I can't see the top. The topography's completely changed, almost instantly, from the flattish lane to the alluring path climbing straight up.

It's exhilarating, beginning to ascend. I feel as if I'm being lifted and the world's getting bigger and wilder below me. It's a passive sensation, as if there's no effort involved in the climbing and the path is somehow carrying me. Most of the many pilgrims I saw this morning are having lunch down in Rabanal, another inviting place of cafes and restaurants designed to appeal to the kind of people that would be walking the *camino*. It has benign New Age atmosphere, like a Spanish Totnes , but with stronger shadows and houses that face inwards to courtyards like the House of Bernarda Alba so that for all I know, behind the hanging baskets and smart front doors, there are rooms full of daughters dying of broken hearts in the face of evil, intransigent mothers. I'd happily have stayed there but I'm saving it for another day.

After a couple of hours of ascent I can see no one. I sit to have my bread and banana next to a water trough, looking back east over the plains leading to León. The view is spectacular and hypnotic. My eyes travel towards and away from my dusty boots to the far horizons, imagining the curvature of the earth along this line of latitude 42 degrees north, crossing Spain via Corsica to Italy, then to Turkey, Georgia and into Central Asia. Then my geography's shaky so I imagine it going west, beyond Santiago and Finisterre and out over the Atlantic to Detroit and Ann Arbor, where it was raining so we dived into a bookshop where you bought me that copy of 'Poets in Their Youth'. My thoughts drift through the places I've visited along that line and people I met there, going up a bit, down a bit. I can sit here forever and lose all track of time. In the same way at home, I sometimes disappear into the atlas and am only dragged out of it by the phone ringing, with a feeling of bewilderment as if I really have been sailing up the Lena to Yakutia, experiencing its sudden spring and explosion of flowers, seeing reindeer herds and hearing the eerie throat singing that produces two notes at once.

Suddenly the lunchers start appearing on the path, interrupting my reverie. Monsieur La Joie is full of mock-superiority at seeing me sitting down. He shouts merrily as his bald brown sinewy legs take him past with no visible signs of effort – 'Auvergne – Un Point, Cornauille – Nul! Ha, ha, ha.'

My sitting here invites comments or concerned questions from every passing pilgrim and it's definitely afternoon, not lunch time any more, so high time to get up and get going. Such prolonged stopping, so lovely for the spirit, is not so good for the body, and all my muscles, from my ankles up my legs to my fat pumping heart deep inside, have to be cajoled and nagged into moving again, without the rocket fuel of morning coffee.

I have the idea of carrying on to a famous hostel, right up on the pass, the highest on the route, which has no electricity. At home, I fantasise about living with fewer things that plug into the wall, spending summer evenings outside, crazed like a Finn by too much daylight and winter evenings indoors in gentle candlelight, so the primitive hostel appeals to me. But I get into conversation with a German woman who has walked the *camino* before. She tells me, yes, that hostel is in a spectacular mountain setting but as well as no power, there's also no running water, just earth closets and dormitories full of the unshowered. She recommends staying in the next village at a convent and leaving the high mountain pass for the morning.

My heart, lungs, legs and feet jump for joy or would if they weren't so weary. It's a relief knowing I'm only going another few miles rather than the substantial ten kilometres or so straight up the mountain to the high hostel. It's a true mountain walk now. We're well above the tree line and instead of a sandy path through scrubby bushes, there's now black rock and scree underfoot and a louring sky above. The little hamlet of Foncebadón, at fifteen hundred metres, has a wild atmosphere. There are falling-down barns and walls, seemingly dry-stone, reminiscent of the Yorkshire Moors. Abandoned farm machinery reminds me of certain parts of Cornwall where a broken-down car or a cement mixer in the front garden are the equivalents of hanging baskets in, say, Surrey. Everything manmade is dwarfed by the massive landscape and looks panicky in the gusty wind – sheets on a line bounce and tug wildly and give the impression of being about to turn into tatters at any point.

The convent is closed. Across the track is a brand new hostel, the Albergue de Monte Irago standing firm and defiant against the rock-strewn landscape. The stones that make up its facade are firmly stuck together with plenty of mortar and it has an emphatic roof that the wind couldn't possibly lift off. It still seems early to check in, only tea time and what on earth will there be to do all evening on the black mountainside with its collapsing buildings and mad wind? The German woman insists. It's one of the few places to stay on the mountain and will soon fill up as people will be more tired than they'd expected from the steep ascent from the valley. With the convent closed and the next hostel even higher, beds will be in high demand.

At first, the *albergue* is unprepossessing. A young woman, with acne, smoking and sulky, takes my name and books me in for a pilgrim's dinner. A baby is crawling on the grimy floor and there are a couple of men wandering around aimlessly. It's hard to imagine what work there is in this inhospitable spot.

The hostels or *albergues* along the route all have different statuses. Some are religious, some are run by municipalities and some are private, either charitable or run on a commercial basis. The cost of a bed varies from nothing or a donation through two euros up to fifteen but this doesn't, as far as I can tell, depend on the services on offer. Tonight's is at the upper end of the price scale.

The dormitory is upstairs and the boot rack is located on the turn in the staircase, where in London flats, people sometimes put in bookshelves. The sight of boots in the hostels is for me one of the great visual pleasures of the *camino*. There's something intimate about the way boots cover what in many people are the two most unlovely bits of the body. They are variations on a theme and comment directly on our differences and our common humanity. To see them assembled, neatly in pairs, big ones, little ones, cheap ones, posh ones, new ones, worn ones, all, it seems, breathing out with relief at no longer being bashed on paths with a great lumbering weight above them pushing them up and down, day after day, is like looking at a symbolic representation of a crowd of people. We are one body because we all wear boots.

The dormitory door has a notice with pictorial 'Forbidden' signs like the old ones in swimming pools saying 'No Petting' or 'No Diving in the Shallow End'. Here, the prohibited activities are Eating, Drinking, Wearing Boots, Filing Your Feet and Cutting Your Toenails. It's permitted to sleep, snore, fart, toss and turn, rummage noisily in bags and whisper annoyingly to friends, and people are already doing those things. They don't, it seems, kiss or pray or sing in the dormitory though those activities aren't forbidden and they may want to.

The room is crammed with beds and the ceiling is low. Being relatively early means I've found a lower bunk in a corner and am able to shower without queueing or hurrying as people are waiting. As there's really nothing to do and nowhere to go, I focus on giving my feet love and attention – without committing the infringement of cutting my toenails – and then washing my clothes in the sink downstairs.

I was emotionally bleak in comfortable Astorga but am content in physically bleak Foncebadón. As I peg my bits and pieces on the full washing line, I clock the corrugated iron strewn around the broken buildings and learn it's an iron-mining area, which seems an antidote to its windy heights, as if the ancient metal anchors it to the earth even while the wind mercilessly shreds the flapping prayer flags someone's tied up here, echoing mountainsides in Tibet. Like the industrial interior of Cornwall, this landscape grows on me. I like the sense of danger in its altitude and lack of vegetation and the fact that in winter, it would be inaccessible. I admire the pluckiness of the hostel owners building so high up in the face of constant buffeting by the wind.

It's still an hour until dinner. I sit outside facing down the valley. My German companion was right, a steady stream of people is checking into the hostel and it will soon be full. I start thinking of hares and tortoises, beginnings and endings, births and, yet again, death. I argue that my fascination with death isn't morbid, even though that's what morbid means. Walking to Santiago is a life in miniature, a lifetime in the middle of a life. We can see what the end of a pilgrimage might be like, look at pictures of Santiago on the web, watch the crazy swinging of the *botufumeiro*, the world's largest thurible, belching smoke like a dragon, on YouTube. But there is still little known or shown about the ending of our longer lifetimes, no one sending postcards from the other side, telling us about delays getting through customs or recommending we take a different route. Simon sitting in Ephesus in my dream doesn't speak to me, to tell me how he got there or what it's like. He just sits, a visitor from the other side, seraphic, inscrutable, dead.

Hamish and Clive and their hurrying come to mind. I think they must be high on the pass in the waterless, powerless albergue and after my shower, hair wash, sock and knicker wash, all in plentiful supplies of hot, clean water, I don't envy them. I want to say that we will all get there in the end, it really doesn't matter how long it takes. Hurrying to Santiago seems almost the same as hurrying to die, as illogical as driving more quickly when petrol is low or typing faster to get all the words in before the end of the line. I'm not sure what difference it makes, ultimately, going faster or slower, or whether we can know until we get there. It's probably good though not to stop too often for too long, to limit the occasions of coming to complete halt at a water trough in a reverie of maps, bread and banana.

At midnight, among the snuffling sounds of forty people sleeping in close proximity, there's a sudden and unexpected moment of silence. The room has become stuffy and someone gets up to lift a blind and open a small window. This action quietens even those people who are fast asleep and snoring loudly. Cold air comes in, breaking over us like a wave on a beach, giving immediate refreshment. The open window frames its bright field of stars and there's peace. We are for a moment one body because we all breath with one silent breath. Then, of course, the silence falls apart, fractured by a bronchial-sounding snore and the creak of someone turning over in the bunk above me.

Chapter Four

A dark time

There are rules in some hostels about not getting up too early and disturbing others in the mornings. They may give precise times and sometimes, doors are locked prohibiting early risers from getting on the road as soon as they can. Someone tells me about a woman who misread her watch, got up, dressed and left her hostel, only to find, once outside, it was only three in the morning and the door had locked behind her. She sat on the step, freezing cold, waiting for dawn. Today, I know it's too early but I haven't seen any formal curfew and I'm awake and eager to get going. I attempt to pack quietly and of course, drop my metal water flask so it clatters over the floor followed by the tuts and turning-over of those still sleeping.

It's cold out on the path, and at this height the stars seem close and appear to pulse against the pitch black of the sky. The path, I recall from yesterday, simply goes straight up, up and over the mountain. It really is dark – I can see bugger all. But I begin to walk, one little step in front of the other and somehow my feet find the path. Theodore Roethke wrote, 'in a dark time, the eye begins to see' and sure enough, I sense the last buildings of the hamlet materialising to my left. I get more confident, start taking bigger steps and the path comes up to meet my feet and the darkness wraps itself around me like a blanket. I'm soon warm in my layers of clothes and from climbing. The stars shimmer, I'm purposeful, strong, walking my way through northern Spain, not afraid of the dark.

It was a different kind of dark, the year I finally left you. Everything was a mess. I thought I'd escape to London for a month in the summer. A much-loved cousin was sharing a rambling Victorian mansion in Brockley, South London, a student-house arrangement, even though the residents were pushing forty and all professionals. They had an empty room, a big garden and there would be congenial company and interesting conversation. I could stay there. A friend and colleague then offered me her Central London *pied-à-terre*, right in the middle of Bloomsbury. I was incapable of making sensible decisions and it seemed the second offer was a special gift and hard to refuse and in bright June sunlight, I entered the darkest phase of my life.

Her small flat is at the top of a tall thin house near the British Museum, an area that's famously haunted. The side streets are narrow, which meant the flasher in the building opposite was only a few yards away so I had to keep the curtains closed along one side. My only responsibility was watering the window boxes and that became almost too much. I was convinced I was either over-doing it or not watering enough and would neurotically check the soil several times a day.

My friend is happily married and the flat to me, smelled of marriage, the mingling of two individual scents into one, that is something like cold tea with overtones of sweat and sex and undertones of love. Their double-bed folded out from the wall and brought down with it all those thoughts of our happiness, your infidelities, our own king-size bed like a raft in the spacious bedroom at the Coach House where we slept easily together, moving in unison like two waves coming slowly onto shore.

In the tiny flat, I changed the sheets and changed them again but the scent of marriage still emanated from the bed. Like T.S. Eliot's yellow fog, it nuzzled the air in the kitchen, the living room, nudging over the window boxes, making me check once again with a finger tip that the soil was neither too wet nor too dry.

And London was stiflingly hot. It took me ages to get to sleep, then the sound of bin men collecting bottles from pubs I hadn't drunk at, woke me with a crash at five am each morning.

Dusty Springfield, who provides one of the soundtracks to our affair and marriage, since we played her loudly in a borrowed Moscow flat on our first trip to Russia, echoed through my mind those during those London days – *I just don't know what to do with myself* in her beautiful plangent tones, my own creaky, miserable response *I don't know what to do, no, no, no* … I hardly knew whether I still had a self, let alone what to do with her.

Books are my default option, where I go for answers, so I walked the hot streets to the Waterstones near University College which had a satisfyingly extensive section on 'Depression'. I bought a self-help paperback called 'Broken Open' and lay on the bed that wasn't ours and wept. It was a kind of crying I've experienced only a few times in my life. Once it went on for a whole day, becoming something other, a possession by a gigantic grief that was unfathomable, oceanic. Fortunately, I was with someone. This time I was alone and thought I'd be engulfed, swallowed into the dark belly of a whale with no human hand to hold on to stop me. The tsunami was approaching inexorably and there was nothing, no branch, no hand-hold, just the up-suck of air before the wall of water would send me flying and I'd sink into black nothingness. This was the end. I was finished.

I sank, yes, but strangely an hour or two later, was bobbing back on the surface. There was land in sight and I hadn't drowned. It made me think of Langston Hughes' 1951 poem 'Island':

Wave of sorrow,
Do not drown me now:

I see the island
Still ahead somehow.

I see the island
And its sands are fair:

Wave of sorrow,
Take me there.

Those moments of going under, disappearing beneath the wave, seemed to have changed and restored me, as if by a total immersion baptism and I felt curiously brightened up, as if I was on a sunny island. I'd been to the darkest place imaginable but I really was still here, with the clamour and murmur of London and a whole world beyond the open windows. How lucky I was to have the use of this flat! It seemed I did still have some wits about me – so I gathered them and thought fresh, new post-almost drowning thoughts. I'd visit friends in London or, even better, invite them round for drinks. I started thinking about where to get ice and what snacks I'd prepare. I'd have a meal and see a film with my best friend Belinda, as we used to in the old days when I lived in London. I'd 'do' some museums, more bookshops, buy some new clothes, make the most of the quiet to finish a project on my laptop.

But, like a rainbow appearing then fading after a storm, my up-beat mood didn't last. My heart wasn't in it. In fact, it was clear to me that my heart was the source of the problem. The pain was there – in that funny four-chambered muscle I carry around in my chest. I could point at it for a doctor and say, 'It's broken.' A far cry from the love-filled passion flower that beat against yours in bed when we'd sometimes steal off to make love in the afternoons then doze in a tangle of duvet and happiness, it had shrivelled in a purple craven thing. Even my pulse felt weak and after that brief recovery, where I could believe for a while I was on a sandy beach, tears, no longer violent or terrifying, just sad, were never far away.

The turning point came later that day. The instinct to run away again, this time to home rather than from it, was turned into a decision by a visit to the Lido in Holburn for a swim. The concrete, the noise, the fetid smell of strange bodies, the claustrophobia compared to a Cornish beach, even Gylly in high summer, turned my stomach. And as for the drinks parties, I discovered most people I knew in London were away or working or busy and arrangements made for the day after tomorrow were too distant – a floating plank out of reach when the currents were sucking me over the rapids.

It still took two attempts before I finally fled. I packed, cleaned and tidied and took the Number 7 bus to Paddington, which gave me a tourist's tour of London for 80p with my pre-Oyster book of tickets. London looked nice – full of interesting people and places, so much more stimulating than Cornwall, and I was due to see Belinda the following day and how silly to rush away. So I got off the bus at Paddington, crossed the road and got on the same Number 7 back to Bloomsbury. I went back to the flat, lugged my bag past the bikes up the steep staircase and opened the door – only to be hit again, violently, by that yellow marriage thing. It wasn't nuzzling now but shoved me back down the stairs, on the bus to Paddington Station and the familiar litany of the Penzance train … Plymouth, Liskeard, Lostwithiel, Bodmin Parkway, Par, St Austell, Truro.

That dithering in those dark days when London was at its brightest couldn't be more different from my steady, thrilled walking in the pitch black up Mount Irago, with no doubts about where I'm going. I'm enjoying this enveloping dark, the crisp air, the steady climbing and more than anything, its certainty. Suddenly in front of me are two dipping and bobbing spots of light, coming from the head torches of a couple approaching from behind. I greet them and receive a ticking off in Spanish from the man in response – it's dangerous to walk in the dark, there are stones and rocks and branches, I could fall and trip at any point. My Spanish isn't up to telling them that life's a dangerous walk in the dark and, in comparison, this plod up the mountain is easy. He repeats the warning and I begin to feel sorry for his companion, imagining her tolerating this prissy bossiness day after day.

Somehow, they stay behind me, and I walk briskly on ahead, beyond their light beams which are disorienting, picking out a boulder here, a bush there and fading out into the empty valley. Then, there's a figure beside me. I've caught up with another person walking in the dark, going at the same speed as me. In spite of my bravado, I like his presence. Manuel is Catalan, probably about thirty, fit and light on his feet. He's walked the *camino* many times. He's friendly, not afraid of the dark.

We pause at the Cruz de Hierro, the Cross of Iron. It's where, traditionally, as pilgrims cross the high pass from one mountain range to another, they leave their old life behind and set out on a new one. The cross at the top is surrounded by a giant conical heap of stones. The custom of adding a stone to the cairn apparently goes back to the Celtic need to propitiate the gods when crossing or arriving at high places. The tradition continued into Roman times when the stones were called *murias* after Mercury, god of travel and communication. Now, the cross is surrounded by all kinds of objects symbolising lives no longer wanted or needed, everything from photographs and little nick-nacks to, I'm told, knickers and bras. It's too dark to check that. People who've walked the *camino*, often mention the Cruz de Hierro as a milestone, one of the high points, literally.

Before leaving home, I'd thought about what I'd like to leave there. I had, on an old key ring, together with my car key and keys to the house I now rent, a door key to the Coach House. It seemed an odd thing to be carrying around with me five years after a divorce and was the subject of much discussion and hilarity at an evening of 'confessions' earlier in the year. Leaving the house, with my rucksack on and ready to go, I decided it was small enough, yet big enough symbolically, to carry across Spain to a high mountain pass and leave on a heap of stones, with other people's old underwear and random memorabilia. But I couldn't get it off the ring and certainly didn't want to take all the other keys. I struggled, employed teeth and broke fingernails but still it wouldn't budge, that silvery, old-fashioned key to your house. I swore and gave up, hung it back on its nail and left.

In Perrault's story of Bluebeard, the much-married nobleman gives his latest young wife a set of keys when he leaves his chateau to journey to the country. The set includes one to a room she's forbidden to enter. Inevitably she does, and finds the remains of his previous wives hanging on hooks, blood everywhere. Blood gets onto the key and can't be washed off so she's found guilty of disobedience when he returns. She pleads for time to pray before he beheads her and is rescued, just in time, by her brothers and sisters, who kill the evil Bluebeard. It's the curiosity of the woman that puts her in peril, as it did Eve and Pandora, but also rescues her from the danger of too much innocence. I completely understand why she doesn't ask Bluebeard about his previous wives. We're all optimists when it comes to love and marriage. If we acknowledged the many and various ways in which men and women might kill each other, or kill off little bits called hope or trust or joy, we'd never take those steps into the darkness of intimacy.

Your relationship history is less fairy tale than a Greek epic where the gods and mortals conspire to create mayhem and madness. Any question I asked that would, for most people, have a simple factual answer, could yield several minutes of back-story, improbable turns of events, explanation and justification. Like Bluebeard, you have a reputation, and when you gave me the bunch of keys, you didn't tell me which rooms should remain locked, in fact you even opened some yourself, to show me blood, complexity, strangeness and sorrow.

And like Eve, Pandora and Mrs Bluebeard, I was curious and couldn't resist that contemporary equivalent of the locked room in the cellar, your computer. I think you half-wanted it to be opened. You were free with your passwords, so that even your renegade son had access and would immediately relay what he'd found to anyone else in the house. Once my curiosity was piqued, I regularly and shamefully read your emails, torturing myself with knowledge, the key becoming more and more bloodstained. I confessed to my priest friend, a worldly resident of Byzantium, who'd flown over to bless our marriage. He was reassuring about my snooping – 'Well, you *are* married' – but unsympathetic about what I'd found, 'You must have known what you were getting into'.

Yes, but not the details. I had a sense of dark cellars in the castle and my own desire to know more about them. When Bluebeard's wife gets into trouble, who's to blame? Bluebeard or her, for being unable to resist opening the forbidden door, or for marrying him in the first place? Or is there a more nuanced explanation, that Bluebeard isn't the wicked man 'out there' but, as in Jung's analysis, the animus of the woman? Could he be her own 'semiconscious, cold, destructive reflections', the feelings 'that invade a woman in the small hours, especially when she has failed to realise some obligation of feeling'?

Your second wife had been a muse to you, but when we met, you were long divorced and living parallel lives. Except, of course, it was more complicated than that. She became ill some years into our affair. In spite of the pain it caused her, you wouldn't give me up. She, in turn, was violent and destructive. It was an intolerable situation and I took a job in Pakistan to put distance between us. But you didn't let me go. In spite of the expense and the time difference, you telephoned me every day, as you had from the day we met, and wrote to me often. It was before the era of cheap calls and your phone bills went into four figures. And, under goodness knows what pretext, you even visited me, arriving bemused in the chaos at Lahore Airport after a long uncomfortable flight.

Our week in Lahore was full of incident and feels dreamlike at this distance. Many people there knew your books and were curious. A young colleague of mine asked you whether you still 'practiced', referring to sex. You replied that by now you were 'quite good at it'. We were almost trampled to death at a holy shrine where opium-addled villagers mistook you, with your white skin and white hair, for a spirit back from the dead. We smoked opium ourselves, you causing hilarity when you kept insisting, more and more incoherently, that it was having no effect, you couldn't see the point. We sat in peaceful gardens amongst dilapidated old colonial buildings, looked at Kim's Gun, so frequently mentioned in Kipling's memoirs and explored the old city, trailed by flocks of young women in bright *shalwar kameez*. Like the old Russia, that Pakistan of the last century no longer exists. Post-9/11, I can't imagine being able to drive myself freely around in an old Ford estate car, travel alone to remote parts of the north, amused at usually being addressed as 'Sir'. As a working Western woman, I was neither fish nor fowl and met nothing but friendliness and gallantry.

To say, it was good of you to come and visit me in Lahore is an understatement. If I ever doubted your devotion, seeing you arrive after such a journey and slip into my life there, it was no longer in question. Rezac, the houseboy employed by my French-Canadian landlady, took a shine to you and every morning would tell you about his 'beautiful dream', that you were going to take him home with you, that he would be able to make your breakfast and iron your shirts in the faraway land of Cornwall, which must be beautiful because of his beautiful dream.

Looking back, I'm in awe of the sheer amount of energy it must have taken for you to keep this confusing romantic show on the road whilst still working hard to maintain your expensive household. Perhaps at that time, we two women were the Bluebeards and you, the hapless maiden with a bunch of keys, not knowing what door you were trying to open.

It's cold up at the Cruz de Hierro and Manuel and I stand stamping our feet, not quite wanting to move on, as if at any minute the peak and its views will become apparent. I imagine leaving my house key here, saying goodbye to it and any fantasy that I can just let myself in to your home one quiet night and wander around unnoticed.

(Strangely, after being with me so long, the key is lost soon after I return to Cornwall, along, annoyingly, with its companion car key, somewhere on Swanpool Beach. The cafe proprietor shows me a whole basin of keys passed on to her by the metal detectors who scan the sand each morning, but mine aren't among them. A week later, I call in again and she says, there's no hope of finding them now, a massive storm has completely rearranged the beach. The key lies now, I imagine, somewhere in the shifting sands of the ocean floor.)

The couple wearing head torches comes up behind us, bobbing circles of light arriving before they do. The man begins listing the dangers of walking in the dark again – *ramas bajas, piedras, rocas … es muy peligroso andar en el oscuro.* Manuel shrugs and greets them in Spanish, saying something I can't catch in a friendly voice that shuts the man up.

I refuse to be frightened when I have my own two feet on the ground, darkness or no darkness. The danger was far worse in that little Bloomsbury flat or when I experienced the vertigo of falling through the floor of my own judgement. I thought that was solid but it could turn to air when you sometimes sat, meeting my eyes and telling me with total sincerity, that black is white, and I hadn't seen what I knew I'd seen. The world of trusting you was full of branches and rocks, yet I managed to traverse it, tripping a little but not falling flat on my face. And, on the other side, there's a beautiful world, a path full of mystery and a place where regrets can be left behind on a high mountain top in the wind and rain.

Manuel's keen to get moving, and gestures with his head. We leave the invisible iron cross and begin a gentle descent. Soon, it isn't dark anymore. A crepuscular light creeps across the mountains, not spectacular like yesterday, but muted, sending a pearliness through low cloud and mist that gradually reveals the path. The landscape seems to be taking off layer after layer of gauze, becoming more defined, like a cleverly-lit theatre set where what at first seem to be painted flats become three dimensional, a vista of high mountains, with a vast expanse of sky.

For a moment, I regret my dark ascent and resolve another year to climb the mountain in daylight, then reprimand myself for wanting to live this moment differently when it is, in the here and now, by any definition of the word, sublime.

The path descends steeply and we come to a road and there, squat against the mountainside in a jumble of prayer flags and painted signposts, showing distances to Compostela, Lima, New York, Peking and London, is the famous high hostel. There's a row of compost toilets near the road and, below, a complex of low wooden buildings, all wreathed in wood smoke. Manuel says it's a good place to stop for a rest and a coffee. We go through an archway and meet two older men, bundled up in jumpers, hats and scarves feeding a couple of braziers, with a few pilgrims sitting around them, quiet and pensive. There's something medieval about the scene – no sign, of course of any power supply and, apart from plastic vats of water lined up, nothing that speaks of the twentieth century. I learn that the silence is because the *hospitaleros* implement a strict 'no-one-up-before-dawn' policy so there's no evidence of the people staying at the hostel. At one point, a woman appears at the doorway and is immediately commanded to go back to bed. No one's allowed to get up before 9am when they will be given breakfast.

So those of us warming ourselves at the braziers have walked here before dawn and there's a sense of camaraderie. Manuel hands me a roll-up and I enjoy its bitter taste and get high on tobacco in the thin mountain air. Two cats rub against my legs and a puppy is making its own fun, playing with a stick in the dust on the ground. When the water boils, I have a cup of instant coffee and struggle to understand the murmured conversation in a guttural Spanish.

The place is somehow disturbing. I know I'd hate to be kept prisoner in a dormitory by these two mountain men, jabbing the fires with their pokers. They remind me of the hostile faces of some of the farmers on Bodmin Moor, where my six month stay cured me of any romance about country life. Driving or walking along the deep lanes, I'd see farmers herding miserable dairy cattle with grotesquely distended udders dragging on the ground, or forcing terrified sheep into pens. I grew to hate seeing men and women on horseback, tight lipped as they yanked the beautiful creatures around with a combination of metal, leather and fear. I was still in a post-divorce maelstrom of sensitivity and although I loved the emptiness of the moor, its dramatic hills, rivers and star-strewn nights with no light pollution at all, the animals broke my heart. Some friends had sub-let me a wing of a Duchy farmhouse, remotely situated at the top of a track from one of the narrow lanes criss-crossing the Moor, with no other houses in sight.

I was lonely and began to bond with the animals I saw regularly. A sow, kept alone in a stable near my back door, greeted me each morning like a dog, wagging her tail, hungry for company and affection. She was pregnant and after giving birth to a writhing heap of piglets, lay grunting and content as they organised themselves to suckle in neat lines. She was later in deep mourning for her young, summarily removed for slaughter, and gave out deep sobbing sighs when I stopped to scratch her head on my way from home to car. I longed to rescue her, to mend her giant piggy heart alongside my own. These men in their mountain eyrie thousands of miles away remind me of the farmers in that stern, unsentimental world of rearing animals to kill for food.

Morning has well and truly broken and the sky's clearing to a matt blue. It's going to be a golden autumn day. One of the cats jumps onto my lap and begins purring and dribbling. I finish the nasty coffee and begin to think of moving on. Manuel and the others are planning to stay for breakfast and one of the *hospitaleros* is setting out bread and jam on a long table. There are signs of life in the dormitory, curtains being opened and faces at the window. The puppy is gambolling around happily, chewing on bits of wood people dangle for its amusement. At one point, it runs towards a brazier. The closest mountain man cracks it on the head with his poker and it stops, stunned. There's a deeper silence in the quiet as everyone jumps at the sound of metal on bone. The puppy looks up, whimpers, then wags its tail, hesitantly. I remonstrate, politely, all the time wanting to say 'you bastard' or the Spanish equivalent. My loathing of those who are casually cruel to animals or children finds its focus on this man, holding court in his high mountain fiefdom. Others, more articulate, join in and someone picks up the puppy to comfort it. The man looks chastened, if somewhat surprised, at the reaction and I suspect that as the puppy grows up, it's going to get it again and again.

The sun's climbing and the mountains are inviting. I set off, wanting to enjoy the cusp of the day, when there's still an early morning freshness and to avoid the probable rush of people from the hostel after breakfast. The path follows a spectacular curving arc along the side of the mountain, with views stretching for miles to peaks every direction and down into the empty valleys. Many miles away, wind turbines catch the light and sparkle like little jewels along the ridges which repeat infinitely towards a hazy horizon. Everything's touched by gold in the clean light and the air has the champagne quality of somewhere totally unpolluted. The wide sandy path cuts a swathe through bracken and thorny bushes, and is easy going underfoot.

I find myself singing again, my small repertoire of songs seems hard-wired and link brain to heart to feet. After a few rounds of 'To Be a Pilgrim', I devise my own version of the Proclaimers' chanting love song: 'I will walk one thousand miles and I will walk one thousand more, to be the one who walked a thousand miles to lie down at your door – na-na-na-na, na-na-na-na …' adapting it like ten green bottles to be a countdown to Santiago. It's still early morning, I'm alone but have been meeting kindred spirits for the past few hours. I've slept, eaten and laughed well the previous evening, enjoying paella at a long table where eight of us had no single language in common, but found each other through wine and jokes that transcended the verbal. I've escaped the horrible mountain top hostel, my boots are comfortable, the air's intoxicating and the whole day's ahead of me. The distance will be easily covered on this wide undulating path, stretching invitingly for miles ahead and trailing behind me, totally empty of people.

Then I look down and am frozen to the spot, feeling the hair on my arms and the back of my neck prickle and stand up on end, in an atavistic and instant sensing of peril. The swift haunches and tail of a dog-like creature that comes up to my waist, are disappearing into the bracken just a couple of metres ahead. It's so quick it might be a shadow or a trick of the light. But the giant paw prints, clear as illustrations in a guidebook, in the sand in front of me, are undeniably real. I'm paralysed and experience for the first time that cartoonish cliché of fear, of being rooted to the spot as the hair on my head lifts skywards in defiance of gravity.

You loved a New Yorker cartoon in which a frightened person is opening his door to an unthreatening-looking man with a folder of papers. The man on the doorstep is saying, 'I'm your biographer.' and the householder's hair is vertical in terror. But this is no biographer, it's Mr Wolf, a creature I've always wanted to see in the wild, but not here, when I'm completely defenceless, in a place totally unlike Moscow or any of those dangerous cities I've lived in, where being streetwise will do me no good whatsoever.

The paw prints zigzag, crossing the path into the bushes, then re-emerging and disappearing at intervals. My heart's pounding and I feel sick. There's nothing to do but to walk on, singing quietly, if rather quaveringly, so that I don't take him by surprise. I wonder whether I should swing my pack onto my front in case of attack, so he'd sink his teeth straight into my neck rather than disembowelling me so I'll be in agony as he tucks into my liver. I imagine an obituary in the West Briton, *Falmouth Woman Eaten By Wolf*, the Facebook tributes, tears, or so I hope, at my funeral and everyone saying, well, at least she died doing something she loved. I imagine gazing into the bright yellow eyes of a beautiful wild creature and yielding to the inevitable. I prepare to give up the ghost and all the many ghosts accompanying me on this walk to Santiago.

For the next few hours, I walk through the golden landscape as if I'm in the Psalms and it's simultaneously a place of milk and honey hewn out of the rocks, where I'm fed and made to lie down in green pastures, and also a valley of the shadow of death. The beauty speaks of goodness and mercy but I'm convinced the wolf is just biding his time before he leaps out at me, clenching his merciless jaws around my head, leaving me limp and bleeding.

So when a shadow creeps out ahead of me on the path from behind and I hear breath and feel warmth, I don't flinch but just say a final prayer of thanks and farewell. But then the wolf speaks, and it's not a wolf at all, but a handsome Brazilian man, loping along with wolf-like grace and speed. We were both sitting in the circle around the brazier at the high hostel and he's caught up with me. I can't stop grinning. We talk for a while and take pictures of each other. The one of me smiling in the mountains is full of relief and joy and excitement. Then he overtakes me, his long strides quickly putting distance between us.

I'm no longer frightened, nor even sure whether my earlier fear was justified or hysterical. All I need for reassurance, it seems, is the presence of another person. Although we're soon too far apart to help each other fight wolves into submission, illogically, I think Antonio, being in front, will be the first to meet any danger. He is the only one to pass me during the whole day in the mountains. For the time being though, I sing my heart out, like an Aborigine singing the path into existence. 'I will walk one thousand miles and I will walk a thousand more … na-na-na-na… nanananana!'.

The path undulates up and down gentle peaks and troughs until finally it reaches the end of a long, slowly descending ridge. Villages and a broad alluvial plane come into view. The villages turn out to be small hamlets, picturesque and deserted with old fashioned houses with room for animals on the ground floor. Every so often there is a new building or a sign to a hotel or hostel or restaurant. I catch up with Antonio, who, like me, hasn't been eaten by wild animals and we sit and drink water at a fountain before he strides off ahead again. The path then veers away from the road and drops steeply through a landscape reminiscent of a Romantic painting of the Dove valley in Derbyshire, all streams and waterfalls and rocky outcrops. Parts are quite precipitous which means a slide and a scramble, using hands and bottom as well as feet. I enjoy the tricky bits, finding them a change from the usual well-trodden path. The foliage has changed and there are glittering willows and bright green and gold shrubs catching the light. 'She'll be coming round the mountain when she comes …'. It's early afternoon and I'm hungry and elated at having crossed the mountains.

Eventually, the steep path meets the road and I'm in the little town of Molinaseca, photogenic and tidy with a two thousand year old bridge and ancient streets. It's clearly a tourist destination. My snatched breakfast of a muesli bar, instant coffee and a roll-up is an age ago, so I stop properly, treat my feet to being put up on a chair and order orange juice and tortilla, sitting outside one of the prettiest bars on a cobbled street lined with cafes. A few other pilgrims drift by, all seemingly as good humoured as me from the stunning day's walk.

Two familiar figures come into view, only they look different. It's Hamish and Clive, who'd propelled themselves past me with their long walking poles, turbo-charged by testosterone on the second day. Hamish is in a state, he's limping, looks haggard and his knees and elbows are cut and bleeding. They join me, order beers, and I learn how Hamish's boots are crippling him. He'd paid a fortune to have them specially made from moulds of his feet to be a perfect fit as he had no time to prepare for the walk. The last rocky bit of path was a struggle, and being tired and in pain, he fell several times. As a tall, big man, carrying a large pack, his falling, I imagine would be like a giant tree crashing down when the woodman's axe severs the last splinters of trunk.

We solve the mystery of how, when they'd taken off ahead of me, they then fell behind. They were asleep in the high hostel where I'd sat that morning. Clive is clearly concerned for his friend and also, I think, though he doesn't say so, at being held back. We still find much to laugh about in that British way that of puncturing a potentially serious conversation with frequent jokes and laughter. The reality of Hamish's massacred feet though, is unavoidable and I get out my collection of foot creams, unguents, arnica, antiseptics and blister plasters, some of which he agrees to take.

The next part of the Way is less spectacular, a long approach to the city of Ponferrada, some of it alongside dual carriageway looping its way towards the town. Pilgrims are numerous now, strangely, given my several solitary hours earlier today. We fill the hard shoulder and accelerate, not just down to the town but towards the end of a long arduous day.

There's a holiday atmosphere. A group of Mexicans is in high spirits, shouting and joking, ill-equipped in well-worn trainers, some carrying hold-alls instead of rucksacks, and few with guitars. We pass a vineyard and one makes a great show of offering me grapes. Sheer gravity carries us onwards, my own legs are wobbly with fatigue.

I choose a purpose-built hostel in a monastery. As we wait to check in, there's celestial music playing on a loop and American women in slacks and full make-up move along the queue with glasses of fruit juice. The registration's slow as names, nationalities and passport numbers are scribed by hand into a ledger and our pilgrim's passports are stamped. The hostel's brand new and up-market. A water feature tinkles in the courtyard, there's a large well-equipped kitchen, library, computer facilities and a careful segregation in the dormitories of women from men from couples. Spotless showers and laundry facilities are on the far side beyond a garden and a chapel. The American ladies glide around like geishas, offering advice on the town, pointing out the facilities in the hostel.

There are two German women in my room. At first, I'm glad to be in a room with just three of us instead of a huge dormitory until, as they've claimed the lower bunks, I find it's a rocking, rattling climb up an unsteady ladder for me to reach a top one. Perhaps they are a couple hoping for privacy as they meet me with some hostility. They're very tidy and the older one tells me, 'I zink you should take your zings off zat chair'. I can see no reason to, the chair's a perfect place to put them out of the way and I can't imagine us wanting to sit on it in the corner of the room. I childishly put my belongings somewhere less convenient for all of us. 'I zink you should put zem zere,' she snaps, pointing to a corner. So I obey, then think I'll have a nap and clamber onto my bunk while they converse *sotto voce* beneath me. Then I need to pee and have to come down again, nearly kicking one of them in the face. There's more tutting and black looks. I get back up again and we all sigh. I'm aware of a distinct and unpleasant aroma and peering down, I see a pair of boots and damp socks. I clear my throat and say in my best RP to the older woman, 'I really think you should put your boots out in the corridor like everyone else.' She glares and I think for a second she might hit me, but she says, 'Zat is a reasonable request,' and picks up her boots. She's now friendly.

Perhaps she sees me as a kindred spirit, one of those people for whom the right thing being in the right place matters a great deal. I wonder what sort of disarray surrounds the Mexicans in their corner of this orderly hostel and remember how happy they were in their shambolic descent into the city.

Ponferrada's post-industrial decay, cheaply built apartment blocks and unprepossessing streets surrounding a couple of ancient squares, remind me of towns in Eastern Europe. The city is dominated by a massive twelfth century castle built by the Templars. They ran it, and the whole city in fact, on behalf of pilgrims on their way to Santiago de Compostela. It looms in the central square like a spaceship, with seemingly little connection to the present community.

There's a tiny church at Temple on Bodmin Moor, dedicated to St Catherine of Alexandria, which was also used as a refuge in the twelfth century. Pilgrims travelling to Santiago, Rome or Jerusalem from Ireland and Wales, would land on the north coast of Cornwall and walk across to the south, to avoid the perilous sea journey around Lands End. The little village of Temple and its church are on one of their routes. Temple, much later, became the Gretna Green of Cornwall, where people could marry without having the banns read for the usual required weeks beforehand. When you first, very early on, decided that you wanted to marry me, we didn't rush off to Las Vegas but you did begin looking out the necessary documents. It was only then you learned that the divorce from your second wife, two decades earlier, hadn't been finalised, that although the *decree nisi* had been duly issued, neither of you had followed up on the *decree absolute*, assuming that the other had done it. The solicitor meanwhile, like a Knight Templar, had gone out of business. Twenty years later you were unexpectedly still married and then, in the fictional way your life unfolds, you were widowed instead of divorced.

I'm not sure where our *decree nisi* is, nor even if I'm entitled to it. When I swore on oath that we'd lived completely separate lives for two years, I was lying and my knees knocked as if there were a savage wild animal lurking on the other side of the glassed-off cubicle, rather than the yawning court official who'd passed me the official words to read and the Bible on which to rest my hand.

I'm on a quest in Ponferrada to divorce my photos from the full memory card on my camera. There's apparently a camera shop where I can do this, but in Groundhog Day fashion, I keep coming back to the same square over again, even though I'm following directions. Roberta, the betrayed and beautiful Italian woman, is sitting alone outside a bar, writing her diary and laughs every time I reappear still unable to shed my photos.

Just as the two books I brought with me have been given away on the first and second day of my walk, and a t-shirt already discarded in a hostel, my camera will soon be posted home. It's become a symbol of a wrong way of living, attempting to fix moments instead of live them, a literal and psychological burden. I've kept just two of my photographs of the *camino*, the one of me on the high peaks and another of shelves in a hostel full of boots at rest, all dusty in shades of grey and khaki.

There was only one photo on display in the living room of our marital home, of your second, deceased wife, radiant and smiling. It always struck me as being for public consumption, like the torrent of poems that spilled from you after she died, re-storying your long and tempestuous relationship, reminiscent of how Thomas Hardy's love for Emma only found its true expression when she was no longer around.

Upstairs in your study, John F Kennedy and Jackie appear in profile in a framed poster of the book cover of your 1992 novel, *Flying Into Love*, tousled, looking heavenward. There are no photographs of your parents who had lived and worked in Hollywood and perhaps the Kennedys are kind of substitute. You often spoke of how your father admired America for its egalitarianism and open-mindedness, even calling the modest bungalow he built on the outskirts of Redruth, *Beverly*, after Beverly Hills.

The other portraits in your study aren't photographs but a reproduction of a painting and sculpture of two Russian writers, who have been your lifelong companions since you learned the language during National Service at the height of the Cold War. Anna Akhmatova, Stalin's half-nun, half-whore, in the 1922 portrait by Kuzma Petrov-Vodkin, looks down at you as you work. Anna is an influence on you in many ways, not just as someone you've translated. You have a fascination for St Petersburg and you even named your monthly writing group Stray Dogs after the nightclub where she performed her poetry. That was before Stalin's Terror that led to the execution of her husband and later, the imprisonment of her son, her own exile and the silencing of her work for decades. The complexity of her relationships finds parallels in your own web of love, marriage, deaths and divorce, real and imagined.

Stray Dogs in Truro is many miles from Petersburg in more ways than one. Our late-capitalist, liberal democracy has little in common with a new country emerging raw and excited from a revolution. In Truro, worries about drink-driving and general health concerns meant that alcohol and smoking were mostly replaced by careful bottles of mineral water and opening of windows. Sometimes, though, the evenings would turn from a polite examination of people's writing to a lively, laughter-filled affair, even dancing sometimes, although not the exotic cabaret of long-ago St Petersburg.

The group had been established for over a decade when I came to Cornwall. I only gradually learned about how the long-standing members were entangled, Bloomsbury-style in different love affairs, some long over, some still going in the form of stolen clinches in the kitchen.

I attended Stray Dogs for the first time when I made the move to Cornwall in the spring of 1999. My friend, Jo and his family, came to stay within a few days of my arrival. By then Jo was 'our friend'. You'd read and admired his book, 'Russia: A Long Shot Romance' and when I intro-duced you to him in London in 1995, it was as if another romance had started. You connected not just over Russia, but shared interests in litera-ture, cricket, history, politics, enthusiastic smoking and, more than anything, singing after dinner. Your joint favourite 'I dreamed I saw Joe Hill last night', sung loudly in the style of Paul Robson with improvised harmonies, was a form of bonding as close as any I've ever seen.

During the first years after we met, we'd often stay with Jo and Yelena in London, in their rented house in Marylebone, sleeping on a soggy double bed in the basement, entwined all night. Their daughter Katya, from age five onwards would improvise dance routines to the Spice Girls, which we'd watch, drinking red wine. We'd then have dinner, the cooking inspired by Yelena's Moscow and Jo's international love of food. Then, you and he would sing, sometimes for hours and to the bemusement of any other guests. Later, when I lived in London, I worked in an office near Regents Park, so I'd pop in to see them often in the same way I used to spend time at their *dacha* or Moscow flat, when I was working in Russia.

When I moved to start my new life in Cornwall, Jo's immediate response was to say, 'We're coming too'. He parented me in many ways – just as he parented his extended Russian family, wife, daughter, step-daughter, mother-in-law and their many Russian friends who constantly needed his help and loved his deep spirit and compassion. He, perhaps like you, was never quite at home in England but in Moscow, blossomed, enjoying the way it was possible to be serious, religious and intellectual whilst still prioritising hospitality, friends and a good piss-up. He unstintingly helped a younger Russian music journalist to get his books out in the UK and the States in the late 80s. The younger man's charm and good English meant he was fêted by influential people in Britain and the growing and dodgier elite in Russia. He was my boyfriend for a while, and Jo strongly disapproved of our relationship, just as later, he was sceptical of my marrying you, although at one time he loved Artyom like a son, and you, I think, like an exasperating brother.

My first attendance at Stray Dogs was helped by Jo reading from his never-to-be-finished novel-in-progress, 'The Russian Bride' and Ksusha, his step-daughter, giving a long and intense account of how she translated Yeats' 'Leda and the Swan' into Russian. I can't remember if I read anything that night. And your Cornwall tribe watched me, those people who knew you well and knew me as 'the other woman', or as I now realise, one in a long line of other women, who would be introduced as 'a student' or 'research assistant'. Six months later, all but one of them came to our wedding and heard Jo reading from Corinthians in his beautiful voice, then joined in the mad dancing in the living room with the chairs pushed back.

After an hour or so, criss-crossing the centre of Ponferrada, I give up on finding the camera shop and go back to the hostel where there's to be a 'Blessing' in the little chapel across the garden. It's a warm night and the tables and benches outside are full of people eating, strumming guitars, writing diaries and winding down after the walk. The hostel holds a hundred pilgrims and only nine of us go into the chapel. The priest appears from a side door in shorts and a well-worn t-shirt. He's self-effacing, softly spoken, moving between Spanish, English, Italian and French as we do, following in turn, the words given on small cards. He tells us that the *camino* is different in the various seasons. In summer, pilgrims are mostly tourists or doing it for 'sport', whereas in winter, nearly everyone walks for spiritual reasons and the chapel is usually full. I suppose September is somewhere between the two. Each of us is invited to contribute something in turn, a prayer, a song 'from your country' or just a few words. I don't understand their words, but feel something give when the quiet voices of the Italian couple who speak first, crack with emotion. When it's my turn, I stumble through a verse of 'To Be A Pilgrim' before my lips quiver and eyes fill. Soon, as we go round the little group, everyone's in tears, and the gentle priest is passing round the box of tissues kept handy near the altar. All I can think of is asking your forgiveness for my leaving you and the forgiveness of all those people who in October 1999 gave our marriage their blessing.

We intended a quiet, modest wedding. You, rather strangely, insisted on buying me an engagement ring. I'm uneasy with jewellery as I seem to lose or break it in inverse proportion to its value, however hard I try not to. When we first met on Skyros, you gave me a silver brooch of a human form, arms crossed, holding a flower. I've only worn it twice in fifteen years, fearing it would fall off and be lost. We didn't buy wedding rings. I was happy to wear my grandmother's and you never wore jewellery. You efficiently went to the Registry Office and booked the earliest possible date. I bought some pre-printed paper with a blue and misty cloud background so that we could make our own invitations.

You wanted a Prayer Book Service. For all your expressed irritation with the Church of England, you love the language of the King James Bible, its connection with Elizabethan England and the time of Shakespeare. But you were divorced from your first wife and there was no way then of marrying in an Anglican church, even though three years later that policy was changed. You made an appointment for us to visit the Methodist minister. You were brought up on Cornish Methodism, knew the hymns by heart and didn't taste alcohol until your first sherry at Oxford. The Minister was warm and welcoming and had no problem with our age difference nor our wanting a religious ceremony. I, though, found myself uncomfortable with the cosiness, sitting in her small living room on a hot day. The floral carpet, the careful cups of tea, the electric keyboard in the corner all spoke of a world like that of my grandparents. I adored them but could never truly be part of their traditional world.

My own upbringing was religiously confused. My parents didn't baptise us, thinking we could choose our own way. My dad was an outspoken atheist, my mum calls herself agnostic yet they encouraged my sister and me to go to Sunday School in the village, perhaps simply to get some time alone together when they couldn't afford babysitters.

Unexpectedly, in my late twenties, in Istanbul, the Great City, I had a conversion experience one Sunday in the Anglican Chapel of St Helena. The Chaplain and I had become close and instant friends after being sat together at a lunch party. I was spending more and more time with him, in spite of my reservations about his day job. He encouraged me to attend the Sunday morning service and I spent it squirming with irritation and impatience at the superstitious mumbo-jumbo. I persisted, though, and went along every Sunday, mostly for the conviviality of lunching with my friend and others after the service. When the first Gulf War broke out, Istanbul, in the Turkish tradition of welcoming strangers that began with the Jews fleeing Spain in the fifteenth century, became the favoured destination for refugees from Kuwait. Many of them were Tamils, already refugees from Sri Lanka with little hope of ever returning home. They were skilled tradesmen and had been working as electricians and builders in the Gulf. Ian took care of them, setting up a makeshift hostel in the then disused Crimean Memorial Church. Many of them would come to St Helena's on Sundays.

One day, Ian invited everyone in church, whether Christian, Hindu, Moslem or non-believer to come to the communion rail for a blessing. I went, with my heart pounding and as I knelt to receive the blessing, there was, as in all those clichéd accounts, going back to St Paul of Tarsus, a blinding light, a sense of the world falling away and from that moment onwards, no doubt whatsoever. I was broken open and felt myself disappear and then, to my surprise found myself still here, still inhabiting a living, breathing, but most definitely temporary body.

I couldn't speak for the rest of the day. The next day, Ian left on holiday to Greece but sent me a letter in which he described seeing a light that was so bright, he nearly dropped the host. We've never discussed it. In spite of a curiosity about other religions and an openness to any ritual that brings me closer to God, I've stuck, considering myself Christian and Anglican, but as I first encountered it in Istanbul, interwoven with the influence of Greek, Armenian and Syrian Orthodox Christianity, Islam and Sufism. In England, I'm most at home with worship in cathedrals with their emphasis on liturgy and the anonymity that wouldn't be possible in a parish church.

In spite of sitting near the back, and never staying for coffee after the Eucharist, I was caught at Truro Cathedral one Sunday as I left and shook hands with the then Dean. He spotted my engagement ring. Congratulations, where was I getting married? I explained that you were divorced, that we were thinking of a Methodist Church but he wouldn't have it – we must have a proper blessing and it had to be where I regularly worshipped. It felt too much, too exposing, but he wouldn't take no for an answer. What made it possible for both of us is that Truro Cathedral, built at the end of the nineteenth century, incorporates St Mary's, the original sixteenth century parish church. St Mary's Aisle is intimate, unlike the French Gothic extravaganza attached to its side. The form of words, though, still exercised you and at our meeting with the Dean, you produced your own version of a wedding service combining Prayer Book with modern sentiments appropriate to a church blessing of a registry office marriage. The Dean was cautious and whilst he admired your creative approach, couldn't risk using an unsanctioned form of words. But you had, mostly, your choice of hymns, Love Divine of course and, Jerusalem, not always permitted but one for you and Jo to belt out. Our joint favourite, 'My Song is Love Unknown', was ruled out on the grounds that it celebrates the crucifixion and is unsuitable for a wedding.

We sat with our address books and the invitations, saying to each other, what with the short notice and the distance, she won't come, he'll never make it, definitely too far for them but let's invite them anyway. The party was going to be at home, cocktail-sized Cornish pasties and sparkling wine from France, our lodger doing the music on the decrepit but powerful eighties stereo. Then everyone started saying 'yes' and could they bring a friend or a cousin, and was there room for kids? And the answer of course was always yes, even though there wasn't room. An afternoon ringing round village halls and hotels drew a blank, so we had a kind of half-marquee rigged up against the side of the lounge and opened the French windows, October or not.

It really was the happiest day of my life and if I'm honest, not because we were getting married, but because nearly everyone I loved was gathered in one place, wishing us well, mixing and blending with your family and friends – who surprised you too by coming from far and wide. Maybe they were motivated by curiosity because it was your first and so far, only, actual celebration of marriage. Your very early first marriage was a traditional family affair and your second and fourth took place privately in the presence of just the required witnesses.

I loved the makeshift nature of it all, how we planned it in a hurry, the way we couldn't find a taxi home after the ceremony and stood in the drizzle as everyone drifted away, how our guests mixed, no top table or hierarchy of invitations to different bits of the day, my sister zipping me into the elaborate girdle I'd bought for the occasion, my glamorous pilot cousin arriving late with a carton of Marlboro as a wedding gift, kids skidding up and down the floor of the marquee, the dancing that got wilder and louder, especially to the theme of the evening, Mambo Number 5, my step-dad having the time of his life, twirling my mum in an incongruous quickstep, seeing Jo dancing for the first and only time, your son's hilarious 'unaccustomed as I am to being best man at my father's wedding' speech, Ian being snogged by a Stray Dog who had been smitten by the way he'd led The Lord's Prayer, the moment in the service where you couldn't read the Post-It note on which the Dean had written the responses and leaned closer and closer, almost toppling over, giving me the giggles, friends coming from China, Germany, France, all so unexpected and wonderful. I say quite often, well, the marriage didn't last, but I wouldn't have missed the wedding for the world.

I learned later that you walked up the aisle with your fingers crossed. And that night, you didn't want to come to bed, preferring to stay with the last stragglers in the living room. I tottered down in my silver wedding shoes to retrieve you but to no avail, so I tottered back up again and fell into a deep dreamless sleep fully dressed and alone. Our honeymoon was a weird one, a few days in Devon, where we made love a lot in a dusty room where a thick curtain of spiders' webs joined the wardrobe to the ceiling. You suddenly produced a Book of Common Prayer. I sat in my honeymoon underwear, promising that I, Victoria Janet Field, take thee to my wedded Husband, to have and to hold from this day forward, for better for worse, for richer for poorer, in sickness and in health, to love, cherish, and to obey, till death us do part, according to God's holy ordinance. And thereto I gave thee my troth.

And here in Ponferrada, in a circle of strangers in a chapel along the *camino*, I realise that I may have given you my troth, but I've taken it back, broken it, allowed it to be betrayed, even though there's still love ten years later. For weeks after the wedding party, the gloomy house seemed lighter and sparkled with the ghosts of a hundred people jumping around to daft pop songs, changed by joy, and I let it go, put it all asunder.

Roberta is among the small gathering of pilgrims in the chapel. We leave together and share some red wine. We don't have enough mutual language to share stories but something's communicated as we chink glasses.

Chapter Five

A hard road

PONFERRADA TO AMBASMESTAS, 30TH SEPTEMBER

This too is beautiful, I have to remind myself, following the Way through suburbs and ribbon development, crossing roundabouts and dodging traffic. These street lamps, these cars driving through the dawn, these pavements, are all fruits of the earth and work of human hands. Lights going on in windows, sparkling necklaces of busy, distant roads, dustcarts and street sweepers moving noisily about their business are integral to the life of this city, where I know no one, where I slept for one night, gave cursory attention to the magnificent castle and am now moving through and away from. This isn't the easily appreciated natural beauty of yesterday's mountains or the picture-postcard prettiness of the town of Molinaseca.

The route goes through the middle of a housing estate of blocks of flats and I can hear toilets flushing and showers running as people wake up and begin their morning rituals. The fabric of the city is made up of the weave of these strangers and their activities, journeying to offices, factories or shops, where they'll connect with others, buy things for themselves and their families, participate in the give and take of commerce and employment.

We pilgrims have abandoned all that. No one's expecting us anywhere today, we have no jobs to go to, few possessions and little connection to the places we move through. Like leaf-cutter ants with our packs on our backs, we blindly follow each other in a line into the west, eating, drinking, peeing, defecating and sleeping en route but connecting nothing with nothing.

Perhaps that's why I'm enjoying myself so much. I've severed so many connections during my itinerant life, moving from place to place, living in different countries, failing to make a permanent homes anywhere, feeling more comfortable with the freedom of renting. This walking, this constant forward motion, makes a virtue of that severing. A pilgrimage means leaving things and people behind. Moving on is what it does.

Ponferrada, and all the other cities, towns and villages along the way, stay put and a river of pilgrims flows through them. At yesterday's hostel, one local man bathed in this river in a very direct way. He'd set up a pair of chairs at the entrance and ministered to pilgrims' feet. Elderly, bespectacled, wearing a baseball cap, he could have been anyone's grandfather, but for his kit of scalpels, scissors, bandages, iodine, oils and plasters. A queue of people waited to sit in front of him and offer him their bare feet, with their blackened nails, bruises and most disturbingly, broken blisters. One French woman had feet that were a mottled pink and red marble of different degrees of skinlessness, a disturbing sight as if she'd been caught wearing her body inside out. The Foot Man was unfazed and ignored her wincing as he gently snipped off redundant skin, mopped pus and stroked exposed pink flesh with iodine-soaked cotton wool. Her blisters were stigmata of a kind and seemed simultaneously a reproach, a reminder, and an echo of Good Friday in these sunny September days. And the man himself seemed to be permanently celebrating Holy Week with his washing-up bowl devotions.

I was next. I had no blisters but my calf muscles had seized up and were hard as iron. He spoke no English but turned out to be a total Anglophile, although for all I know, he may have loved France, Brazil or any other of the countries represented just as much. As he pressed and kneaded my legs so precisely and firmly that I wanted to squeal, he told me about his son in London and his many visits to Khide Parrk and Bookinkham Plas. To my surprise he knew Cornwall through its most famous author, one whose books had been serialised on TV, but whose name eluded him. I guessed Rosamund Pilcher but he shook his head, sending me through a list of others – Daphne du Maurier, John le Carré none of which were right. We changed the subject. He didn't want payment, this was something he did in his retirement as a gift of service to the *camino*, he liked to help. By the time he'd worked his way down past my ankles and was pulling and wiggling each of my toes, the name of the writer dawned on him, Rosamun Peeelcha! That's what I said, I said, but he shook his head denying it, and the massage came to an abrupt end. Sip some water every kilometre, then your muscles won't tighten, he told me and I discovered he was right. As he dried my feet tenderly, I felt the whole of my body respond with echoes of how, once, the feet of St James had been washed and wiped by the towel wherewith He was girded. I stood up on my reborn legs and allowed the next in the queue to offer him their feet.

When I think back on the *camino*, and how my feet served me so well, I recall how they passed not just along the paths and roads, up and down hills and mountains and in and out of hostels and cafes but also through the old man's warm hands, and how tender yet confident he was with his intimate touching of parts of me that were painful and tired. He must have cherished hundreds of other feet so that in all our moving along, many of us are connected by his loving touch and desire to serve. We are one body, albeit a strange one with our tens of thousands of feet carrying us along to Santiago.

Eventually, the town peters out into some ribbon development and then the Way makes an abrupt turn off the road onto a track leading through vineyards. It feels like I've left a city in Eastern Europe and have arrived in the South of France. There's a light drizzle and the earth smells fecund and sweet. Joy bubbles up and I find a new song to sing at the top of my unmusical voice, 'If you're going to Santiago, be sure to wear some flowers in your hair, if you're going to Santiago, you're gonna meet some gentle people there.'.

There are once again mountains on the horizon, dark and purple-looking against the red earth and the greens and browns of the vines and the gold flashes of birch trees changing colour. My inner chatter quietens now it's no longer competing with traffic and I yield to the beauty of the landscape, seeing it through the lens of Cézanne and Van Gogh. You and I went once to Provence, to the wedding of my friends' daughter. The trip was relaxed, free of any tension. We stayed on the top floor of a converted watermill where a constant breeze fluttered the curtains, and you were loving and attentive. There were wedding guests from all over the world, many like us making a holiday of the trip. We sat in village gardens, drinking wine from early morning, enjoying the lavender fields and little villages. The wedding was dreamy in a romantic ancient church where an unaccompanied choir sang and the bride's uncle recited poems in

English and French. You are often prickly and hostile in company, disliking having to play any role or feeling uneasy away from the home where like ivy you're rooted in the walls by tiny invisible suckers. But there, in the slow Provençal summer, you mellowed. It helped that you could smoke everywhere, the weather was *doux*, the scenery ravishing, the wedding party and local French were so welcoming. It would have taken a massive effort to start an argument on say, the EU or one of your other favourite hobby horses.

We took our time driving slowly back from Orange to Nice, staying one night high up in a remote pension against the Mont St Victoire, the mountain that Cézanne painted obsessionally, at least sixty times. The mountain remains the same yet in every painting it's different, seeming to flicker and change with the subtle use of a little more red, more attention to the diagonals, the addition or omission of a tree that dramatically alters the perspective. Pasternak wrote of poetry as needing music, painting and meaning. I could change this account of my past by adding more or less of the red, black or yellow that makes up the mountain of our marriage. I remember that particular trip in the pastel colours of a quiet happiness and, apart from one hill-top town on market day which was over-run by British tourists, empty places and an easiness between us.

With hindsight, I wonder now whether you were between affairs so that I wasn't picking up on the subtle electricity of the excitement and guilt you emanated when there was a new liaison in the making. Or perhaps, it was just a question of light and weather at that particular point in our relationship, which made the landscape sunny and inviting instead of a complicated mass of purple and grey brush strokes.

The path undulates through vineyards, doubling back through an abandoned village, and the landscape becomes gradually tidier as I get closer to the day's destination, Villafranca del Bierzo, home to a cluster of monasteries and ancient pilgrim's hostels. Signs begin to appear advertising restaurants and hotels, and eventually, one saying only 1km to the town centre. I've learned not to trust these. Distances are as shimmeringly imprecise as the idea of a single mountain called St Victoire. The last kilometre to somewhere is always longer than the first one out of it and those in the middle change length dramatically in proportion to tiredness, hunger or thirst.

This last kilometre into Villafranca today is at least five long and takes ages, but it's downhill and the ancient town, nestling as ancient towns often do, in its hollow with mountains all around, is unspoilt and inviting.

On the way down, three men ask me to photograph them at the Puerta del Perdón, the entrance to a large Romanesque church. This is the place where sick or injured pilgrims could claim their *compostela* without having to walk any further. It's tempting to hang around and talk to the friendly young Spaniards but I passed through some Gate of Forgiveness in the little chapel last night and today, for once, don't feel in need of shriving.

Villafranca's a beautiful town and it's lunch time. I sit in an open air restaurant in the main square at the same table as an attractive Swedish man in his sixties, who'd been in the hostel last night, then at my coffee stop this morning. We have lots in common but his legs are twice as long as mine and once the caffeine had worked its way through me, I struggled to keep pace. So we said farewell and *Buen Camino*, and he hared off, loping like a blond Ethiopian into the distance. I didn't expect to see him again and yet, tortoise-fashion, I've caught him up. We talk some more while he waits to pay his bill and I order. Then, his long legs unfold themselves like a giraffe's and he towers over me, wishing me well once again and is gone.

Each of these partings is like a mini-version of someone dying, especially those deaths where someone simply goes off stage and never returns. If you don't know the play, it's only at the end you realise certain characters have just disappeared. On the *camino*, and in life, there are so many conversations that are only started, all conversations on the frontiers of dreaming where now, I remember little of the content, only the connection. Several months later, and I can't recall his face, only brightness in a smile and the presence of a tall, blond person with whom I connected. Everything's gone but the essence, like a song heard once on the radio where the title, artist, lyrics and melody fade but the feeling it generated somehow contributes to this joy that fuels everything, like an invisible wind sending a boat towards harbour over a bright blue sea.

Egg and chips and a Coke. Childhood pleasures. And then, astonishingly, like a risen Christ, Hamish of the ruined feet and injured legs appears in front of me. How on earth has he caught up and where's Clive? It turns out Hamish has taken a bus from Ponferrada to Villafranca, is planning to meet Clive for lunch, then go by taxi to a hostel five miles or so further along. He's relaxed, enjoying what's now a holiday without the pressure of keeping up with his energetic friend. He's seen a doctor and a physio and is strapped up and dosed up. He's now acquired his own apothecary so returns my various foot ointments.

There's a mini-phrase book in one of the guide books to the *camino*. There are none of the old chat-up lines such as 'Can I offer you a drink?' or 'Would you like to dance?'. Instead the useful phrases offered are addressed to the doctor or pharmacist. 'My blisters have burst.' 'I am constipated.' 'My lower back is in spasm.' I imagine Hamish had made full use of these.

The next part of the *camino* is the most testing for me. I didn't see that there was a mountain route to the next village, arduous probably, but I imagine beautiful, full of the scents of low bushes and herbs. I like sensation of climbing high, boots knocking against rocks on a steep path. Instead, I end up on the low road which then funnels itself into a deep pedestrian way next to a busy carriageway sweeping along the side of the mountains. It's truly dismal, an endless whoosh of cars behind the concrete barricade to my right and only little glimpses of woods and a river over the wall to my left. And there's no escape, once in this container for walkers, for ten long, tedious miles. Someone has graffitied a series of commands on the pavement, accompanied by cartoons for a mile or so. Jump on the spot! Sing a song! Dance in a circle! Touch your toes! They break the monotony but the joke soon wears thin.

Eventually, there are small detours through the tiny villages where the old road must have passed. These are quiet at siesta time, just a cat licking its bottom in the sunshine, an old man dozing in a chair in a porch, no shops or cafes, no signs of purposeful activity. One place has a tiny hostel, just twelve beds or so. I see Roberta sitting on the steps waiting for it to open. She asks me to stay too but it's early in the day and I don't want to stop where birdsong's drowned out by the intermittent roar of the main road behind the village.

Around tea time, I get to Trabadelo and plan to stop at the hostel there. Hamish and Clive have already arrived and claimed the lower bunks their height and size require. The French woman with the unspeakable blisters hobbles past in flip flops, carrying a bundle of dripping laundry. She's like a modern San Sebastian with dozens of invisible arrows piercing her feet and instead of blood a trail of soapy water. Her smug husband came over the mountain leaving her to make her painful way alone along the main road. How she can bear to continue puzzles me but I suspect from her glazed smile she's high on painkillers or suffering, or both.

The three Spaniards, one in a trilby, I photographed in Villafranca are there too and want to be friendly. They must have sped over the high mountain path as I left them enjoying beer and tapas in the square in Villafranca and they didn't pass me along the road . We all sit drinking tea on the terrace and I taste my first Torta de Santiago, a kind of Bakewell tart dense with almonds, decorated with a cross,. It should be the pleasant close to a long day's walk but the terrace looks out on an intersection of two new 'N' roads and we have to raise our voices over the sound of lorries decelerating on and off the slip roads. Hamish tells me, it's all going to be like this now, from here to Santiago. My heart sinks, though fortunately, he's wrong. It's still only around five and my little leaflet says there's another hostel six miles or so further on. I um and ah and eventually fill my water bottle, tighten my boots and once more put on my rucksack, leaving the others busy getting the beer in while I walk away in order to escape the noise.

I'm tired though, and a few hundred yards down the road regret my decision. The traffic noise, rather than diminishing is getting louder and more bothersome the further I walk. Freud despaired about what it is that women want but maybe discontent stems from a conviction that things can be made better. At home in Cornwall, I complained about your wanting to stay indoors too much, that we didn't share enough outside interests. The one time we went to a beach together, all you wanted to do was sit on the sand, togged up in your warm clothes and smoke. My fantasy of near nakedness and swimming entwined in the water was never even a possibility. After my sulking on Gyllyngvase Beach, we never attempted 'outdoors' together again, other than sitting in beautiful pub gardens.

You went to every match Redruth rugby team played at home on Saturday afternoons throughout the winter. I accompanied you only once and at half-time, when the novelty had worn off, was cold and bored. We never attempted rugby together again. I went every Sunday morning on my own to Mass at the cathedral and never thought of asking you to come, although friends who were staying with us usually accompanied me. Like the couple on the astronomical clock we saw in Prague, we went in and out of the house at different times, watched carefully by Tamsin the dog.

I can see the village I'm trying to reach but have completely lost the Way. There are no yellow arrows for several hundred yards in front of me, just a chaos of roadworks, complicated contraflows, a stranded petrol station and lorry park with no obvious route for pedestrians. It's hazardous in the extreme. I dodge huge lorries and pick my way through churned up earth. and criss-cross the road-in-progress, futiley looking for arrows. There are uprooted trees and the mountainside has been torn open with the beginnings of a vast tunnel for traffic. In my diary I've written, dramatically capitalised, The World Is Being Raped. At one point, I walk through a scatter of bright poppies sprouting on upturned earth, reminiscent of those that flowered in the trenches of Northern France. Alongside the digging to my left is a small river, its banks somehow unviolated, lined by trees turning gold and rosebay willow herb, wild strawberries and some dandelion type flower, diminished by the noise and chaos to my right, but beautiful none the less.

I'm almost exhausted when I escape the chaos and reach La Portela, another small village turned into an island by the new road development. There's no sign of the hostel. I walk the length of the main and only street to where an old woman and two young men are sitting on a wall. I ask them, I think in reasonable Spanish, where the hostel is, and they respond by cackling, pointing every which way, up the street, down at the ground, up at the sky, behind each other's heads, laughing maniacally, showing rotten and missing teeth, looking at me with a combination of menace and lunacy.

I retrace my steps and cautiously enter a large public-looking building, only to be chased out by a woman wielding a broomstick. I've walked into a Jerzy Kosinski story and it's only a question of time before I'll be tied up and fed to the dogs, or have my head shaved and be dunked in a manure heap. I sit despondent in the church porch for a few minutes trying to decide what to do. There's a hotel back at the road junction but I can't face crossing that traffic again.

There's nothing to do but to carry on another five miles in the hope of a hostel that actually exists. I steel myself to run the gauntlet of the three crazies sitting on their wall but they've mellowed and instead of shouting and cackling at me, they smile gappy smiles and theatrically wave me on my way. Perhaps they've done their bit, making me feel too unwelcome to stay in their village.

There's more motorway, then mercifully a bifurcation where the asphalt and roar of engines take off towards a giant flyover connecting two mountains. I follow the left hand fork down a little lane alongside a river towards Ambasmestas. It's dusk and there are cows ambling through water meadows and a fresh scent of foliage uncontaminated by dust and fumes. I've walked twenty four miles today, propelled by a kaleidoscopic mixture of enthusiasm, joy, frustration and determination. My feet are on fire.

When I take my boots off and peel away my sweat-sodden socks in the cosy little hostel, I see my feet are coated in minute blisters. They are as small as pinheads and have formed at each of the many hundreds of points where the weave of my socks meets my skin. I stare at them for the rest of the evening in fascination and by bedtime, they've disappeared like stars do at dawn.

Antonio, the Brazilian I'd met in the high mountains is in the same hostel and gallantly offers me his lower bunk when he sees me baulk at climbing to the upper one which has no bars to keep sleepers safe. That automatic action of caring and generosity reminds me of parenting but of course it happens in male-female relationships too, not least in the way my step-dad took care of my mum. But I always find it surprising when someone is unexpectedly kind, thinking 'it's my job to be kind to them!'. Many people assume I married you looking for a father figure and I'm sure there's truth in that. My own own kind and loving father died of a brain tumour aged only forty two. If Freud's compulsion to repeat is to be believed, I've also been attracted to men who keep an emotional distance, who, like my own father just when I needed him most, won't be there for me.

On our first research trip to Moscow, in 1995, when we were together for only the second time, we sat, coincidentally, in the Spanish Bar, one of the few non-Soviet restaurants in the city at that time. It was tucked into a corner of the monstrous Hotel Moskva, where every facade is differently grim, allegedly because Stalin ticked his approval on a whole sheet of designs rather than selecting just one and the architects were frightened to tell him. You asked me to give an account of my romantic history, insisting on detailed answers to your questions. Now of course, I'd tell you to mind your own business, but then I was in thrall to you. Getting people to talk and to disclose, is something you are good at. Your beautiful voice reeled me in, as in the lines from Othello you often quoted, like a falcon with you holding the jesses to stop me flying away. When I described the relationship I had in Turkey with an actor, and one in Russia with a writer, both public figures, you called me a 'star-fucker'. I'd never heard the phrase before and was shocked, both by the language and the unfamiliar concept. They were simply two men I'd met naturally through friends and something began between us. Of course, sexual attraction is largely unconscious, a process of recognition, whether, as Freud would have it, of family dynamics, or of something more mysterious and karmic. My merchant seaman father was born and died in the same years as Elvis, and is prematurely up there in the field of stars. You too are born in 1935, only a few weeks before my father was, and sometimes, during our early years together, I felt a mutual tenderness that was parental as well as romantic. When we were trying keep our connection post-divorce, you had the bizarre idea that you might adopt me, but when you enquired, it turns out there's no such provision under the law for an adult to adopt another adult.

The pilgrim's dinner on offer at the hostel is a meaty stew and I'm too late for a vegeterian alternative. I case the few restaurants and cafes in the village. Only one kitchen is planning to open and not before nine thirty. So I sit outside a bar in the cool evening air and dine on a bag of crisps and two glasses of Rioja, enjoying salt and oaky tanin on my tongue and lips. I look up at the night sky, and think of the beauty and ugliness of today's walk as a living metaphor of life's journey. I'm alone and romantically unattached, and rashly feel I can fall in love with each and every one of the stars above me and have that love reciprocated a million-fold. The wine is working its wonders.

After the star-gazing, I look down again at the constellations of minute blisters now fading on my prickled feet. I'm in awe of the whole hydraulic and mechanical miracle of these small, sinewy, bony protuberances propelling my body along all those miles.

Chapter Six

Up and away

The road out of Ambasmestas is dark and deserted when I leave the hostel before dawn and I'm wary of missing a turning onto a path or track, but soon straggles of pilgrims emerge from hostels further along, light from their head torches bobbing up the steeply climbing lane as if we're on a stairway to heaven.

The next village, Las Herrerías is a rural, stony affair, and is the gateway to the mountain path that climbs up to O Cebreiro and into Galicia. Its name refers to the steel industry and the scruffy village has the tough exterior that means business rather than tourists. Suddenly, the steady uphill becomes an almost vertical ascent, leading into woods of gnarled oak and chestnut. I've had a coffee and croissant at a roadside cafe and yesterday's long trek was followed by a dreamless sleep and I have no trouble climbing. In fact, I'm elated by the effort and attribute my high to endorphins, whilst having no real idea what they are.

I stop to rest at a point in the woods where the path changes direction, affording new and precipitous views down the valley. An elderly Japanese man pants and mutters his way towards me from far below. When he reaches me, he bows and I bow and he bows again a bit lower. He introduces himself as Ishikawa and tells me today is his seventieth birthday. I'm impressed and congratulate him. We both bow again before I continue, leaving him resting where I was sitting.

The path grows even steeper. Every so often, gaps in the trees reveal deep, romantic chasms and increasingly panoramic views over the province of León I'm leaving behind. Eventually, the Way opens out from the woods onto a farm track along which are big yards and outhouses, each guarded by a massive lump of dog, powerful-looking beasts somewhere between an Alsatian and a Pyrennean mountain dog. Until today, the only domestic animals I've seen along the *camino* have been cats, all gentle, some friendly, mostly content to ignore me and continue washing themselves in a patch of sunlight as I walk by. These dogs, untethered, bark loudly and rush backwards and forwards, slavering and growling. It's only by reminding myself that people constantly, and I assume safely, walk past them that I find the courage to keep going.

When I first arrived at the Coach House, one dark winter's evening, your little Cairn terrier Tamsin yapped in excitement the other side of the door. I'd always been nervous of dogs and asked 'Will she bite me?'. It was a ridiculous question. She was a loving and characterful dog and devoted herself to each of the three women you were married to during her nineteen year long life. I was only ever briefly a Mrs Thomas, and happily went back to my maiden name when the bank told me I couldn't be one customer and keep both names. For Tamsin, I think all the Mrs Thomases were one continuous being, and she showed the same extravagant affection for us all. Your cat, Lucina, was elderly and in that pipe-cleaner stage of a cat's life, with thin grey fur over a spine knobbly with protruding bones. I was still heart-broken over the premature death of my own much younger, plumper cat and disliked Lucina rubbing her boniness against me, purring and dribbling. I'd sometimes push her away impatiently. You reprimanded me sharply, one of the very few times you ever did, saying that she might not be the most attractive cat but she was one you loved and would I please respect that?

I liked you telling me off, justifiably holding me to account. I was uncomfortable with your permissiveness towards me, and your elder son especially, thinking it showed a lack of interest rather than a genuine concern for our well-being. I wish you'd stood up to me more often, telling me to like it or lump it when I criticised, instead of backing away into lies and evasions.

You claim to be a cat- rather than a dog-person but looking back, Tamsin was definitely your familiar. You talked of the need for people to have companion animals as 'guardians of the instincts' and certainly Tamsin knew your every move and would pine if you left the house for more than a few hours. She was attuned to your predictable rhythm, especially meal times and evenings by the TV, but more than that, her reliable, undemanding love for you balanced the more complex needs of your wives.

There was a summer of harmony in the middle of our marriage. I'd introduced a sweet-natured new rescue cat, Daisy. A friend gave me four hens as a birthday present and we kept them free range in the garden, only closing them up at night. All the animals would gather if we sat outside on a warm day. The dog, overheating, would lie on her side in the sun, Daisy would roll in feline ecstasy in the dust on the hot paving stones, Fat Hen, Freckles, Brownie and Nervy pottered about, scratching in the dirt and crooning. My mum and Harry, my step dad, staying with us, marvelled at how the dog didn't chase the cat which didn't chase the chickens, and how their daughter, after all those decades of roaming and failing to settle, was anchored in this domestic sea.

The farm dogs in Spain seem a million miles from that Cornish Eden but on reflection, their attachment to their home and desire to challenge strangers are exactly the qualities Tamsin showed. It's usually taken as a joke when I say 'My ex-husband got custody of the pets' – but it was painful to call in sometimes and see Tamsin's joy at my return and then dejection at my leaving. Daisy was noncommittal and would watch me inscrutable from the shed roof.

The hens all died one by one before I left and we both missed them. You were especially taken by their chatty busy-ness. Perhaps they reminded you of the cake-baking and gossiping Methodist ladies of your childhood in a Cornish tin mining village. At one stage, the hens became a nuisance, getting through a hedge into the neighbour's tidy garden and eating his bedding plants. I wanted to get a run for them, but you couldn't bear the idea of animals, even hens, being in captivity and instead spent a fortune on chicken-proofing the boundary between the houses with a vast quantity of pond netting. The average cost of our eggs at that time was about fifty quid, delicious buttery eggs we'd occasionally find on the kitchen dresser, laid by one hen who would come in through the cat flap to roost on the shelf between the cookery books and bread baskets. You recall those hens often in your poems and I wonder if for you too, they are the symbols of our short-lived domestic harmony, with their generous and characterful ways, their busy and happy colonising of the house and garden.

And my step-dad, Harry, who loved his holidays in Cornwall, talking to you about the cricket and making us all laugh with his stories and sheer love of life, has also died. I'd dreaded telling him we were parting as I knew he was fond of you and enjoyed your long hours talking at the kitchen table. When called him to say I was getting divorced, he took the wind out of my sails by saying 'Congratulations, darling, he was always way too old for you'. Other people, some I barely knew, burst into tears at the news. Just as we couldn't predict how dogs, cats and hens might get on, there's no way of knowing what people really think of a partnership or its ending.

Just below the summit, I come to La Laguna at 1100 metres and stop for an early lunch at a makeshift cafe. I watch familiar figures approaching. There's Antonio, the kind Brazilian, Mr Ishikawa, still muttering, his coat flapping as he walks, and stoical couples, often with one looking longingly at the simple counter, the few plastic tables and chairs set out in the muddy, farmyard-smelling settlement, and the other saying, 'No, come on, O Cebreiro, a real place, isn't far away'. I feel lucky to be on my own, identifying my own needs and desires, fulfilling them or not as I choose. Margery Kempe and Egeria both understood that pilgrimage is a private affair. Even though it's sociable and both women met other pilgrims, guides and sought out priests, monks and nuns, their main aim was to find themselves closer to God, their Christian faith enhanced, by proximity to holy places and relics. I wonder if either of them were ever wistful, like that buried part of me, thinking it would be nice to have someone sitting opposite, digging his fork into our shared tortilla.

Intimacy means, for better or worse, boundaries blur. Sometimes, I didn't know whether I was really happy or the fact that you were happy was making me happy. Eating was one manifestation of this. At home, we ate traditional meat-based dinners as that was what you not only enjoyed but insisted on. Once when you visited me in Chester and I'd made a vegetable curry, you went out for fish and chips afterwards as you hadn't had a 'proper' meal. And yet, it's intensely pleasurable seeing someone enjoying food I've prepared. More corrosively though, I allowed your happiness to become mine in our sexual life, allowing you to use your age as justification for an assymmetry when it came to giving and receiving pleasure.

It was such a gradual diminution of my personal erotic life in the face of your larger and clearer demands, that for years I wasn't aware of it. I often thought I was fortunate having a husband who continued to be sexually alive when some of my girlfriends complained of drifting unhappily into sexless marriages and partnerships. You have what's described as an addictive personality, perhaps most manifest in your smoking. sometimes absent-mindedly lighting a cigarette whilst the one's still burning in the ashtray, and you were compulsively sexual too.

Some of it I welcomed as part of the adventure of our relationship. One of the most content, strange and exciting times was the year, we shared a lover together.

The man in question was young, intelligent, attractive and married and had no desire to leave his family. Like you, he was libidinous with an itch he couldn't scratch. Perhaps one day, someone will discover a genetic basis for being highly sexed as well as other personality dimensions such as a short temper or the religious impulse. Or even an interest in competitive sport, which for me is far more mysterious.

The affair faded naturally and easily. I haven't seen him for years but the affection I felt for him still remains. The experience shifted my thinking and opened me to new possibilities for living and loving which I would liked to have explored with you, even perhaps, that of us living with another man. I have no interest in an open marriage or promiscuity and my tentative explorations were as much about ways of loving and creating an environment that might nurture a more generous intimacy than what sometimes seems like the exclusivity of a one to one relationship. When he left our lives, it was back to me focusing on pleasing you, in order that you might be able to please me, except we never got beyond the first part of the deal.

These aren't things many people talk about but I suspect from the few people I confided in, such experiences are not uncommon. Adultery is one the staple plots of literature and soap operas in all cultures and seems to elicit knee-jerk reactions in otherwise imaginative people. There's a prevailing myth in Britain and North America that an extra-marital affair inevitably leads to heartbreak or domestic disaster and a disapproving disbelief that people in France or Italy might see things differently. I know the truth is complex because, for me, your affairs didn't end our marriage and in some ways I even admire your energy and ingenuity. When yet another female friend tells me of your sexual overtures, I can see that such an impulse might be, as well as the habit of a lifetime, a vote for autonomy and adventure, and perhaps even a version of my own unquenchable thirst to see new places, to put on a rucksack and walk.

But for a marriage to survive serial affairs, there has to be some other form of fidelity to act as the glue holding two people together. I imagine it as a respect and a love that can contain the paradox of wanting autonomy for both partners and simultaneously embracing dependence and sacrifice. Incongruously, the Clintons come to mind. But society, and maybe especially your generation, straddling the repressive fifties and the liberal sixties, still operates a double standard with a distrust of independent women, tending to see them as victims, destined for a life of loneliness, or else a threat to the male prerogative to be both secure in a marriage and a philanderer. Fewer sexually adventurous women seem to be married. At the risk of entering a hall of mirrors, I experienced a misogyny in you that meant you allowed me to allow you to obliterate some of my essential self, the part that not only wanted to give you pleasure but also wanted to explore her own untapped potential for joy. After travelling with you for so many years along the road you chose through the yellow wood, I ultimately became bored and repelled. I saved intimacy for another day and took another path, marked self-preservation. Whether it's as just as fair or just as dark, or will make any difference ultimately, I can only sigh and say I don't know.

There were many tears, before and after our divorce, as the ground between us on which we'd built our marriage collapsed like disused mine workings in Cornwall which can suddenly sink when there's heavy rain after a dry period. The local paper regularly carries items such as: 'Two pensioners ... were woken by what they thought was thunder to find a 15ft-wide hole outside the front of their bungalow at Ashton' and I awoke one day in our shared bed, knowing that it was over. My desire for you that had fuelled all that love making over the years, had simply disappeared, in the same way the rotting timber of an old mine working sinks into the mud and becomes part of it. I couldn't breathe, I had to go. As I write this, there's news of the death of an eleven year old girl on the beach at Perranporth. 'She was exploring rocks with her family when she fell into an adit – a disused entrance to a mine – and landed in a water-filled cavern below ... ten years earlier a woman in her 50s fell into the same opening while on holiday ... and suffered a broken arm and a punctured lung'. I was naive when I began exploring some of the dangerous caves of your erotic world, and, fortunately, stepped back before I fell. I didn't die, nor even sustain serious injury but learned enough about the unstable earth beneath our feet to tread more carefully, to know where I start and stop. It was time to redraw those inadequate maps of dangerous openings and unmarked caves. Finally, I chose to leave the country where such maps are needed.

After La Laguna, I soon arrive at the high point, at 1300 metres, of O Cebreiro, the first village on the *camino* in Galicia. Galicia, like Cornwall, is a Celtic country, distinct from its larger non-Celtic neighbour. Like Cornwall it has its own language, local saints and curious place-name spellings and, in common with the other sea kingdoms of the West, a version of the bagpipes. O Cebreiro is a popular tourist destination. Unlike the place I'd stopped at for breakfast, with its scruffy farms, manure heaps and crowing cockerels, O Cebreiro is sanitised. The granite and slate houses are characteristically round or thatched, pre-Roman and even Stone Age, and all are pristine. Many are now museums, shops or restaurants, themed with stone-age or pilgrim para-phernalia in the uniform good taste that characterises National Trust properties in England.

I buy some beautiful postcards but there's nothing as useful as stamps. I consider looking at the ninth century church but instead stop to talk to Mr Ishikawa who is lunching in one of the big tourist restaurants, marooned on a medieval-style chair at a medieval-style table, a lone diner in an establishment clearly set up for coach parties. His English is halting and I'm disappointed, as I want to find out more about how and why he's on the *camino*. I know in Japan, there are many Buddhist and Shinto pilgrim routes but that Christians there are mostly recent converts and Evangelicals rather than Catholics.

I've been intrigued by Japan since going on a 'pilgrimage of reconcili-ation' in memory of my step-father in 2005, the year you and I divorced. Harry's suffering as a POW under the Japanese was such that, like many other survivors, he boycotted everything Japanese and couldn't bear to be around Japanese people. But instead of a legacy of bitterness, the expe-rience had given him an infectious love of life, 'Because I'm here, darling, because I'm here'. He worked in the Kwai jungle in Thailand on the Death Railway, alongside another internee, the cartoonist Ronald Searle, who recently turned ninety and expresses a similar attitude to living intensely, saying he drinks good champagne every day. Harry, knowing he was towards the end of his life, decided to donate his camp memorabilia to the Imperial War Museum and at a reception there, he and my mum met Keiko Holmes, a Japanese woman living in London who has devoted her life to helping FEPOWS visit Japan. She set up a charity called Agape to free them 'from their bondage of sorrow and bitterness'. Within ten minutes of talking to her in a queue for lunch, my parents, who'd usually take a package holiday to the Mediterranean, had signed up to go to Japan at a fortnight's notice. Keiko's formula for reconciliation worked like a dream. Harry returned full of funny stories about the strangeness of Japan and anecdotes about his travelling companions, and also the story of the moment when he could finally forgive, when a little Japanese girl sitting next to him on the bullet train spontaneously took his hand and smiled up at him, and he realised he couldn't blame her for anything. He came back looking lighter and younger.

Agape allowed family members to go on the pilgrimages on a paying basis and Harry wanted me to go on one too, so that we could compare notes and share impressions. In the middle of those difficult years struggling in my own emotional jungle, I put it off and soon it was too late. He became ill at Christmas 2004 and died a few weeks later. Having survived starvation as a twenty year old, he chose not to eat for the last weeks of his life. My delayed pilgrimage to Japan turned out to be *in memoriam* of funny, dapper, life-loving Harry.

It was totally different from this walk to Santiago. The countryside, the beauty, the companionship of strangers, the meditative pleasure of walking and the steady progress to a destination, makes this pilgrimage a recreation in the serious sense of the word, recreating the self, moving forward into the future. The pilgrimage to Japan, though, was a deliberate journey backwards into some of the darkest areas of the participants' pasts. There was only a handful of FEPOWs, three upright, smartly turned-out gentlemen, well over eighty, and a woman in her sixties. She'd been a child internee and witnessed the repeated rape of her mother, vicious beatings and the suicide of a woman prisoner, pregnant by one of the guards. The rest of us were either widows or sons and daughters of FEPOWs. As Harry's step-daughter, I was by far the youngest in the group. The issue of forgiveness became complex. The dignified, elderly men seemed able, at long last, to let go of their war-time memories.

Perhaps at their advanced age, they were ready to let go of many things. They seemed genuinely in the moment, enjoying being the centre of attention when TV crews and journalists appeared as we visited their various places of imprisonment, factories, hospitals and camps where they'd lived and worked. They appreciated the love and care that went into honouring both their past and their current needs. The grown-up children of the FEPOWs, too, were helped to make sense of their fathers' stories by visits to these places, once scenes of horror, now often peaceful corners of provincial towns. One man was the son of the then Anglican Bishop of Singapore. When the city fell to the Japanese, the bishop was viciously tortured, yet found it within himself to forgive his tormentors at the time of his agony. I was astonished to learn that this saintly churchman had been known to beat his own children for what seem to me minor misdemeanours.

But for the widows, it was a different story. Their husbands had come back from the war often not speaking of their experiences. Previously kind young men returned angry, volatile and prone to nightmares. These women had spent decades supporting their damaged husbands and, I sensed, putting their own needs on hold. In many cases, the men's identities were enmeshed with their service history, so they belonged to associations and attended memorial and other events which was how Keiko knew of their existence. She described how at first she would be boo-ed and heckled when she tried to explain her mission. They sounded very different from Harry, or indeed Ronald Searle, who after liberation, moved into new lives abroad and didn't mix with former service personnel. Drawing a line under the horror and refusing to adopt the role of victim was perhaps the secret of their love of life in spite of the trauma they'd experienced.

The widows were undertaking this pilgrimage without their late husbands, who would never have contemplated going to detested Japan. They were accompanied by the ghosts of these men and were trying to see it through their eyes, wondering whether they would ever be able to forgive.

As we visited more sites, gave talks in schools, churches, at dinners, the FEPOWs grew in stature with the film star attention. Some of the children, especially the son of the bishop, became comfortable taking centre stage and talking about their parents, but the widows shrank into the background, almost collectively, becoming like a Greek chorus in a tragedy. They talked to me not so much about Japan and our immediate experiences as their own private, unwinnable wars, those times when they comforted a grown man who once again had woken sweating, sobbing and screaming in the middle of the night.

I was spared the dilemma of whether I could forgive on behalf of another wronged person because Harry had already done it so clearly on his own pilgrimage. But I was grieving too, for Harry and also for my mum, widowed for a second time, and felt guilty about my failed marriage, which seemed in this context to be due to my lack of what in the war would have been called 'mettle'. Those widows had stuck out their marriages to men who were difficult and demanding. They just 'got on with it' to use a phrase common to the wartime generation. The process of the past being constantly relived during that fortnight touring Japan was exhausting for everyone.

A moment of catharsis came at a formal dinner near the end of the tour. The woman who'd witnessed such horrors as a girl had become increasingly closed-in and expressionless, as if her memories were too much to bear. Through the tireless research of Agape, she was at last able to meet the descendants of the one prison guard who'd shown kindness to her and her mother. He saved their lives by smuggling them extra food, at huge risk to himself. Another FEPOW described the summary and public execution of another guard who gave a group of prisoners a whole chicken on one occasion. Her tears and smiles on meeting this gentle family, who brought photographs of the good Japanese soldier to give her, and the latest little baby for her to hold, were like the sun coming out after six decades of rain, sun that shone all the way home to the UK. After so many dreadful stories, tears, acres of war graves, the horror of Hiroshima, the poignancy of the elderly monks who prayed throughout the war, at last we saw goodness visible when the life of the Japanese family met the life of the British woman.

Close examination of trauma is one route to healing, but this journey in Spain encourages the opposite. It seems to be taking me away from pain and unhappiness. Thinking about sad events through the prism of this walk, changes them. Memories are given new shapes by rhythmic, meditative walking. The vast natural beauty around me in this high mountain environment dwarfs the small matters of my individual losses and disappointments. I'm diminished, and in a good way, by the clear sky and the limitless views across Galicia. The Helen Shapiro song, 'Walking Back to Happiness', accompanies me down the hill from O Cebreiro where the sunshine and the champagne freshness of the air are exhilarating. I can only remember the refrain, which goes round and round in time to my boots hitting the tarmac as I descend, 'Walking back to happiness, woopah oh yeah yeah, Said goodbye to loneliness, woopah oh yeah yeah.' I'm flying.

As well as singing after dinner with Jo, you loved it if someone came round to bash out 'songs from the shows' on the untuned piano that belonged to your parents. Whenever we travelled to something like a festival, on one of the evenings, after a substantial amount of wine, you would reveal your singing voice as if it were a magician's rabbit. 'Old Man River' would come out of nowhere and you'd surprise people with your rich tenor. One Christmas, at the Nine Lessons and Carols in Truro Cathedral, the place where the service was originally invented, heads turned as you and a young woman in front of us, who was a part-time opera singer, riffed on the carols, enjoying yourselves and each other while the rest of us warbled sheepishly into our song sheets.

In the series of increasingly panicky letters you sent me when it became apparent I really was moving out, and your Canadian girlfriend was likely to take my place without you having much say in the matter, you write that you miss hearing me sing around the house in a voice you describe as 'sweet but often off-key'. You'd grown accustomed to it, you say, echoing another song which you sometimes sang to me at the kitchen table.

Here on the open road, where there are no passers by, I let my voice become as raucous and off-key as it wants. Having so few words to play with, I sing them in silly voices, imitate you building up to a warbling crescendo and laugh at the 'whoopah oh yeah yeahs'. With you, I was self-conscious and only joined in quietly, if at all, but out here, my lungs fill and I sing my heart out. I give voice to all the joys that have built up through this walking, feeling sorrow blowing away in the sunny air to some distant place of clouds and rain. The word, I suppose, is 'rapture'. Yet that term for spiritual ecstasy comes from the same route as 'rape' and can also mean 'seizure' or 'kidnapping'. Perhaps such joy can only come out of previous sadness. Perhaps Harry wouldn't have been so acutely aware of the wonder of being 'here' in his eighties if he hadn't woken up day after day with dead bodies of his friends beside him.

The road continues skirting the mountain from where I turn off onto a sandy track, looking forward to an early stopping place after yesterday's too-long day. I walk for a few hours with a woman called Kathleen from British Columbia, who's been ill. She's slower than her companion who will be waiting for her at Alto do Poio where I, too, intend to stop. After some small talk, we find a shared openness to religious and spiritual ideas and are soon exchanging experiences on a deep and personal level. She's probably ten years older than me and I enjoy meeting women of that age, seeing models for the kind of direction I might follow in the coming years. I like the fact she's sensible-looking and has a proper job. I have a prejudice that often exotic-looking people are dull inside, less interesting than those who present with a conventional exterior. Perhaps it's simply that they can't live up to the promise of their appearance.

I'm impressed too by the sheer effort she's made to reach Spain. It's an expensive adventure, to fly from the west coast of Canada. Her long trans-Atlantic hours were followed by budget airline connections to Biarritz and then a journey overland to their starting point of St-Jean-Pied-de-Port. She injured her feet and knees on the first day during a sharp ascent followed by an equally steep descent, bashing her toes against her new boots and of course, there was never time to recover fully. She also caught various bugs and even now, is nursing a cold. I wonder aloud whether Kathleen's psyche is working something out through these minor illnesses. She isn't averse to the idea.

As we approach Alto do Poio, there's another almost vertical ascent up a zig-zagging path. We can see buildings on the skyline so there's a clear goal, but, after the long climb this morning, it's a tough call to find the energy for this unexpected climb on a now baking hot afternoon.

I over-heat and reach the top beetroot-red and exhausted. I see instantly that the hostel is horrible. It's on a main road and consists of a windowless basement extension to a restaurant, dingy and full of grotty looking mattresses too close to each other on the floor. If I slept in a far corner, I'd have to pick my way over other sleepers to get up in the night, or, in a space near the door, they'd be stepping over me. Once again, I've arrived thoroughly tired at a place I don't want to stop at.

Kathleen's friend is there, waving to us from the terrace as we make our laborious plod up the escarpment. She tells us that she doesn't like the look of the hostel either and takes Kathleen to check out the hotel opposite. I decide to sit down and have a breather. The restaurant is packed, inside and out, with a mixture of pilgrims and people arriving in cars to eat, drink and enjoy the view. It's the first time I'm properly aware of cyclists doing the *camino* and guess they took detours around the various mountains. No ordinary clothes for them, it's definitely 'sport' rather than 'spiritual'. They arrive brightly clad in lycra, expensive sun-glasses and ski-style lip-salve. Their cycles are lightweight and gleaming, with gears clicking tickety boo, pristine, well-balanced panniers and saddles in disturbingly surgical-looking shapes. Everything's fit for purpose, like the well-oiled machines of their riders. These glossy cyclists, all French, I think, are part of a large, strung-out party as each arrival and departure involves a loud exchange of *Bonjour, Ca va?*, and *mwah, mwah* on both cheeks. These greetings are invariably followed by a recap of who is still behind and who's gone on ahead. The cyclists' glamour makes me feel frumpy and the bikes too seem to be sneering, implying that walking on paths is cumbersome and primitive compared to the swish of rubber on tarmac. I order the least elegant thing on the menu, coming as I do from the famously unstylish British Isles, a *Caldo Gallego*, the traditional Galician soup, and put my feet, in their cheap and nasty boots, up on the chair opposite.

As well as the noisy cyclists, there's plenty of other activity. A large white-haired man is holding court at another table, surrounded by the debris of his long lunch, empty plates, torn crusts and splashes of red wine. His ample belly is squashed against the table and his face glows with wellbeing. Lots of people greet him and he banters happily with the restaurant staff. Some pilgrims sit down at his table and take a glass of red wine and there's much enthusiastic hugging and thumping on backs. One man turns to me, all smiles, saying, 'This is Miro! He was the first person I met on the Camino ten years ago – and here we are again!'. It's not clear whether Miro recognises the man after a decade, as he gives the same benevolent smile to everyone. He looks like Raymond Briggs' Father Christmas, with his perfectly round ruddy face, fringed with a white beard, and his apple cheeks.

It's fun watching these exchanges as I plough through the comforting soup, with its potatoes, cabbage, green beans, onion and, I suspect, bits of meat as it has a greasy sheen that only comes from boiling bones. It gives me sustenance, though, to carry on, to find a more appealing place to spend the night. I'm relieved to move away from the hubbub of the restaurant onto a quiet grassy path that meanders easily along the long ridge down the other side of the steep hill. I'm slow though. It's been a day of mammoth ascents and I hoped for an earlier stopping place. I start compiling more *camino* aphorisms to go with 'the last kilometre is always longer than a kilometre'. Today's is, 'if you arrive at a hostel at 5pm, it will always be horrible'.

Somehow moving on in the hope of something better is easier than stopping to make the best of what is. Lakes and ponds are beautiful but unless rivers or streams flow in and out of them, they become stagnant, foul-smelling and die. My body, like all bodies, is in constant motion, even at rest. Not only is it moving inside its bag of skin, lungs filling and emptying like bellows, blood and other fluids on their mysterious and private journeys, but the whole thing's capable of forward momentum. Inside, I'm a pile of bones and a heap of sloppy organs. Somehow, the bones are cunningly attached by a series of elastic bands of varying stretchiness – muscles and tendons. The organs are mostly stacked up behind the protective cage of the ribs and skull and the whole lot is run through, like a new house, with plumbing and electric wiring. This strange caboodle is coated with lard and upholstered with variously textured skin. Windows are installed in the form of eyes and some decorative touches added, such as hair on the head and in the crevices, toe and finger nails, eyebrows and the like. And somehow, this bag of organic matter propels itself along, like a Heath Robinson invention, upright in defiance of gravity, all balanced on those size three and a half boots.

And it's not just my carcass that is moving, fuelled by hearty soup, even now being processed into a chemical solution in that bag of acid called my stomach, as oxygen pumps through my heart and lungs, but my thoughts too are coming along with me. As the days pass, I'm more aware of what feels not like the ghost in the machine but a whole host of them, as if I'm a version of the famously haunted Pengersick Castle in Cornwall. I know dualism is out of fashion, but my body and mind feel distinct, if not entirely separate, not least because I can see my body and sense it in space. When we meet and sometimes touch someone, even if they are usually shrouded in clothes, it is bodies that do the encountering, unless of course, we are dreaming or seeing a ghost. Much of what goes on inside, I have to take on hearsay but I can relate to bodily processes such as breathing, blood circulating, the business of digesting food and drink, and imagine the interior activity of my kidneys busy filtrating that earlier coffee and my liver breaking down the slick of grease on the top of the soup I just ate.

The location of my mind is another matter. That I was in danger of losing it in London in 2004 suggests it's one entity, but I also get a sense of the drunkenness of it being various. Is the mind writing this different from the one that dreamed last night of a man's dry kisses or remembers lighting incense at a temple in Kyoto? The poet Les Murray has written about us having three distinct selves: a body, a waking, logical mind and a dreaming, unconscious mind, all of which interact in subtle ways, especially in poetry. As far as I can tell, my various minds don't sweat, get out of breath or require massage, even though I experience effort and release when completing even a simple Sudoku. Unlike my mind, my body has the reassuring continuity of a physical object in the world. Apart from the, thankfully few, accidents I've had, it changes only incrementally, being much the same as it was an hour ago, swelling and subsiding over days and weeks rather than minutes. The task of meditation is to still the mind, shut up all those selves who jostle for my attention, elbowing thoughts out of the way before I've finished with them. But, whilst meditation is calming, I'd hate my mind to be permanently stilled. The constant change is like a river of thought, moving along with all its debris on top and life within and beneath. And at the end, I suppose, it will meet the sea, an oceanic eternity where all those different bits of me will be like the waves, there, then not there, formed, broken, reformed then broken again, by the wind.

There's a poem I return to often, 'The Guest House', by the thirteenth century Sufi mystic, Rumi. Thanks to contemporary translations by Coleman Barks and Robert Bly, he's one of the best-selling poets in the world today. As I walk, I experience the metaphor of the poem as a reality. I'm a guest house, where emotions and memories wander in and out at will, making themselves at home. Some cause me a bit of trouble, others brighten the place up. Perhaps I need some security, a locked door, or a couple of bouncers to check them over.

Besides my multiple selves there's also something other, outside of my making, that I can only call the presence of God. Prayer, meditation and walking give me glimpses of something I can't easily put into words. God takes different forms and shape-shifts in a way that has a dream-like logic. This presence can be frustratingly elusive, appearing like a deer in the woods might when I'm looking the other way, and then, when I spot her, leaping away white-tailed into the dappled shadows. Sometimes I think it's just my imagination, tricks of light inside as well as out in the world. At other times, as it was in St Helena's Chapel in Istanbul, or once, strangely, just walking along Church Street, Falmouth on an ordinary winter evening, there's absolutely no doubt. The veil lifts and a presence floods the world and, even though it's fleeting, I'm sure it's real. God is a clumsy word for its various guises.

On the *camino*, one day God seems to be Light, a birch tree in its autumn colours aflame, another day, Love, suffusing the whole world through the smile of a stranger and, now, the Joy of walking along a wide undulating path on a warm evening in Galicia.

As I muse on all this, a man overtakes me. He's accompanied by a graceful lolloping dog, wolf-like but light on its feet, tail and ears pricked and alert. The man is tall and skinny, wearing red cut-offs and a straw hat, no shirt or shoes, just a tiny rucksack on his back. The track's flinty and rough underfoot even in boots, but he glides past me on his clean bare feet, with a friendly nod and disappears into the distance. He seems free of gravity, unburdened, as if not of the earth. Immune to the sharp stones, he hovers above the path. He's Mercury, Hermes or some other winged god, with his doggy familiar. My practical mind wants to know where they sleep as hostels don't admit dogs, and how he manages with so few things, but I try to silence it, to become light like him, and float along in the sunshine, the beauty, the wonder of a body in motion.

Chapter Seven

Wild nights

I'm in a bottom bunk, thankfully. When I arrived, the hostel was virtually empty but now every bed's occupied and the enormous single dormitory is like a zoo, only one where they've mixed up mice, elephants, snakes and tigers and made them all sleep in one enclosure, extra-close together. The hostel's purpose-built and has a Wild West feel. It's a long, low, wood-clad building and one of the few with stables for pilgrims travelling with horses. The bunks are custom-made out of logs with the bark still on, and are more ample than I need, with plenty of room for the long legs I don't have, or for thrashing around in sleep, which I don't do. But they've skimped on the height, so I have to remind myself not to sit up suddenly but first raise a hand so I don't crack my head on the bunk above.

Now, the whole heavy structure is vibrating in the way a ship does, sitting with its engines running on calm water, with a low rumble that makes me nauseous. The man sleeping above me is the prize specimen of this zoo. He's part gorilla, part rhinocerous. He's the size of a tank and snores like a plane taking off every ten seconds or so. He, lucky man, is fast asleep.

I'd seen him at the pilgrim's dinner in the hostel canteen, a late-middle aged German, giving the impression of *leiderhosen* even though he was conventionally dressed. He's tall, wide, jowly, heavy, solid rather than fat, and was sitting with his son, a mini-me, in his early twenties, less jowly and with more hair. They were a self-contained pair, not joining in the jollity around the table. The son was solicitous, passing plates to his father and filling his water glass. I'd seen him tucking into seconds of soup, seconds of pasta and seconds of Torta de Santiago, not to mention a few pints of beer in the hostel's bar. So not only is he tired from his walking, but he's full of food and drink and deep into a contented, rumbling slumber.

I've seen, in a magazine's problem page, advice given to a woman sharing a bed with a snorer. The suggestion was to try to synchronise her breathing with his, as a way of lulling herself to sleep. I remember thinking it was the thin end of the kind of wedge in which every aspect of her life might eventually be synchronised with his, in order to achieve harmony. I've seen it happening to friends, this lulling, sometimes aided by drugs or alcohol, more often just from the busy treadmill of work and domesticity, especially when there are children. Synchronising not just one's breathing, but one's whole being with the needs of small children, is a necessary fact of life, not an option.

I'm desperately tired, so even though the man above me is a stranger, and we are not sharing a bed in the conventional way, I try to time my breathing in and breathing out with his. But he's having a laugh. Just as I get it, and feel I might drift out of consciousness into the Land of Nod, he suddenly changes his rhythm, so my carefully calibrated out-breath is interrupted by his harrumphing and snorting and sometimes, wild rocking of the bunk as he heaves himself to one side and then the other.

Psssst. Fuck, I think, what now? It's the Brazilian woman in the lower bunk next to mine who, until a few minutes ago, has been texting under her sleeping bag, the phone creating a weird light, like that I imagine emanated by Our Lady at Lourdes, or the long-buried bones of St James before they were dug up in Santiago by a pious shepherd. She points at the bunk above mine, nodding meaningfully. 'Yes, I know!', I smile and grimace in response. She mimes poking up through the mattress which is protruding through the slats of the upper bunk, not far above my face. I make short, sharp pokes but he's so heavy, my fingers meet a solid mass and I'm unable to achieve the strong prod that might make him roll over and sleep more quietly.

In the bunk on my other side, two French women I'd sat next to at supper start giggling. One clears her throat, 'Cough cough'. There's no reaction above so she does it again, emphatically, sharply, 'COUGH, COUGH'. Amazingly, it works, and the giant above me murmurs something incomprehensible and begins breathing loudly but not at the pneumatic-drill volume of before. There's a silent thumbs up from the

French woman, and on the other side, the Brazilian does a triumphant little dance, still lying in her bunk. Then there's the sound of another text coming in, an electronic tinkle that cuts through the crowded dormitory like some kind of shock so people wake up and tut, and there's a multilingual muttering of disapproval. The Brazilian isn't fazed and disappears into her sleeping bag to read what's just arrived. Her companion above her leans down and whispers something and the phone, glowing like a rectangular firefly, is passed up to her friend for her to read the message, and then back again. The upper-bunk Brazilian has long hair, and as she leans down, it drops like a curtain, smelling disturbingly of shampoo, tobacco and foreignness.

We are too close, all of us, far too close, in this huge room of strange animals. The text is clearly exciting as they are both now smiling and squeezing themselves with pleasure. I'm curious and wish I knew what it said.

The Brazilian women start whispering again. Someone from a far corner shouts loudly, '*Taissez-vous!*', which wakes up yet more people, including my bunk-mate who yawns and stretches above me, rocking the bunk again, making me want to weep with fatigue and frustration. He tries going back to sleep on one side and the bunk rocks to starboard, he turns over, so we tilt port. Eventually he settles on his back and the bunk steadies to an even keel. Within a minute, the pneumatic snoring's started up again. If I look one way, I see the French women giggling and trying to catch my eye. On the other side, I think the Brazilian woman on the bottom bunk is having phone-sex by text, so I avert my eyes. Then people start getting up to use the bathroom. The thin door means every human sound is audible. The flush needs several clanking pulls to get it to work, and the cistern takes a gurgling age to fill up.

I check my own phone, which I keep in my money belt inside my sleeping bag. There's no sexy text for me, but I'm appalled to see it's not even eleven o'clock. It's going to be a long night.

The next day, I set off early along the deep lane and enter cow-country. The walk becomes a kind of hopscotch, as I jump, placing my feet carefully around the cow-pats. As the dawn light brings the world into relief, I hallucinate faces in the wet, round deposits along the Way. I'm watched by two alsatians and a terrier as I walk by and when a four-wheel drive trundles through the village, the three dogs leap up to chase it in the opposite direction, yapping and barking furiously. When it's gone, they gallop back to me, looking immensely pleased with themselves as if they've done a good job, protecting everyone from intruding vehicles. Last night, I'd named them the Happy Dogs, having watched them monitoring every coming and going in the village, like curtain-twitching neighbours. When the cows were driven home, bells clanking around their sad necks, herded by two boys on bicycles, the Happy Dogs became hysterical, barking and joining in the herding. They didn't settle until the last straggling cow was out of sight. Job done, they piled on top of each other in their sunny spot at the roadside, mouthing and gnawing at each other, until the school bus drew up, eliciting more barking and chasing before they once again resumed their vigorous love-in at base camp. They seemed to have discovered Freud's formula for a happy life: meaningful work to do, and the company of other dogs to love and annoy.

At Triacastela, named for its clusters of ancient chestnut trees, I catch up with Miro, the *bon viveur* I saw at the restaurant yesterday. We breakfast together near an especially ancient tree, like something from Enid Blyton with its knobbly branches and whorls. According to a sign, it's at least eight hundred years old. Miro tells me that he's walked the *camino* twelve times in the past ten years, in fact he virtually lives on it, returning to his flat only to upload photos and videos to the internet, or to travel to pilgrim conventions in other countries. He writes down for me the words of the pilgrim song he got us to sing last night in the hostel. There were perhaps fifty people round the canteen tables, joining in and improvising percussion with cutlery and water jugs. He adds his hotmail address and tells me, he has a surname but prefers to calls himself Miro Peregrino, Mr Pilgrim. I consider creating an alter-ego as Vicky Pilgrim and quite like it, but decide to save it until I've completed at least one walk to Santiago. In return, I write down for him the words of John Bunyan's hymn.

The pilgrim's song is simple, It's a repeating chant, or a prayer to be said to a rosary. '*Acogenos Senor Santiago, acogenos Senor Santiago, en el Camino a Compostela, Senor Santiago acogenos.*' The word '*acoger*' in Spanish is a rich and nuanced one and suggests holding, protecting, carrying, taking, picking up and transporting, all those things that one hopes a parent or lover will want to do.

Your early letters to me, although Spanish isn't a language you know, carried many overtones of the verb, 'acoger'. On the Greek island where we met, one of the many dramas during that intense fortnight, was another holiday maker having a psychotic episode. The course running in parallel with yours on creative writing, was called 'Manage Your Career'. It sounded like it would be a safe fortnight of practical activity, such as writing cvs, and possibly a rather dry way of spending a holiday. In fact, it turned out to be a far more risky two weeks for the participants than the creation of stories and poems. The subtext of 'Manage Your Career', as we discovered from our communal meals, is 'What Have You Done With Your Life?', a question carrying an implied freight of regret, failure and wrong turns taken. The woman who found it all too much was a previously articulate graphic designer with her own successful business. The day after she went missing, she was eventually located praying and madly gesticulating in a NATO barracks in the military zone on the far side of the island. Her valiant boyfriend made the complicated journey to Skyros from the UK to accompany her home. You alluded many times to that incident in your early letters, writing that if I ever went crazy on a faraway island, you would, you really would, without hesitation, come get me, '*acogerme*', bring me home, look after me, restore my sanity. You loved me that much.

Now, through my own decision to leave you, it's not clear who would be the one to drop everything and make the journey to bring me home if I was ever found mumbling and raving on a faraway island, or even in a hostel in Galicia, where I'd been driven insane from lack of sleep. I've no husband, no partner, my mother's getting on, my sister's busy and I've no grown-up children (in spite of the mysterious way more one person has asked me how my son is). I have wonderful friends but who would know how to find them if I was suddenly moved to walk miles across a rocky landscape to pray for a group of bemused Greek conscripts? I'm on my own with St James, asking him to '*acogerme*' to Compostela, beautiful luminous St James, courtesy of his accolyte, the self-created living legend of Miro Peregrino.

Hamish and Clive roll up to the cafe. I haven't seen them for two days and had no idea whether they were ahead of me or behind. They're sceptical of larger-than-life Miro and sit at their own table, apart from us, with British-style reserve, to have breakfast, nodding across to me and raising their eyebrows.

Unusually for the *camino*, there's now a choice of routes, one via a famous monastery at Samos and the other through woods and villages, along quiet lanes and farm tracks. I decide on the road less travelled by and take the right hand fork from the village. Immediately, I'm alone, no other pilgrims are in sight, there's no traffic, no houses, just a gently ascending lane with a stream beside it. The frothy foliage along the verge is at the tired stage of early autumn when nature's ready to give up all this mellow fruitfulness with a sigh and relax into winter. But the countryside this morning is alive with birdsong, and the clattering warning cries of blackbirds intermittently announce my passing there.

It's idyllic, easy walking and the lane eventually goes through deserted hamlets with shabby houses, chickens scratching in the dirt and potatoes piled up on the open lower floors ready for winter. The fields have been abandoned and unharvested cabbages bolt extravagently on tall knobbly stalks. The unfinished harvest and no villager in sight could have seemed melancholy, but instead, the overall feeling is of restfulness. Something's been accomplished and now it's time to let go, to allow the hens to burble happily about, picking up plentiful seeds and the field to celebrate having more cabbages than were needed.

Somehow Clive and Hamish are in front of me again. They probably passed when I rested chatting to a young German couple at a spring coming down from the woods. I hear them long before I see them, as their walking poles are thrust rhythmically against the tarmac and noisily propel them up a long hill. They tell me the sticks make walking more efficient by ten per cent, or maybe it was thirty, but the increased efficiency comes at the price of a driving, clattering rhythm of metal on tarmac, drowning out even the blackbirds. I let them go on ahead and am once again in the kind of country silence that's alive with creatures who don't talk, but whose presence enfolds me in a sense of connectedness as I walk, so that some inner landscape starts to move outwards.

I can hear how crazy it sounds when I say that on these lanes and farm tracks, skin, the final frontier of myself begins to dissolve and whatever it was that makes me a body apart, disappears so I'm at one with the landscape. Such mystical experiences are so close to madness, it feels risky to share them. This morning, I'm not thinking about those individuals who've died but have the strong sense that all my beloved dead are collectively walking beside me, not talking but being utterly themselves. They aren't of course here in body, nor as ghosts in any conventional way, but I perceive them as a presence that envelopes me in their various forms of goodness.

Especially real is my paternal grandmother, who loved her two grandaughters, my sister and me, with an unfathomable depth. Her love becomes a kind of cushion or magic carpet that I float on, elated. I'm no longer walking so much as being the walk, except the walk, the presence of love and the light in this corner of the world, are all one. The tracks and lanes continue to meander through a landscape that becomes increasingly gentle and soft, opening out into a wide valley and eventually, with signs of habitation in the distance. The morning has turned into afternoon and the early freshness has evaporated in the increasing warmth. I don't want to stop, ever. I'm in a world entirely composed of light and love, my body's an irrelevance, so that instead of walking I'm experiencing the lane beneath my feet rolling away behind me. Transport is the right word here in its many senses. I'm being carried from one place to another, conveyed, moved to strong emotions, getting carried away, enraptured. The world is becoming one, and not just 'world' but everything beyond it too, the blackbirds, high clouds, people I've known and yet to know, the cow parsley, a silvery stream. Past, present and future become an irrelevance, everything's rolled into one with this motion of walking.

Since, I've wondered why I had those sensations at that particular point of the walk. There are theories that our early landscapes influence our psychology more than we're aware, and the scenery of today's walk is reminiscent of my undramatic childhood landscape of East Kent. But more and more I find that psychology, although helpful, isn't sufficient. The way the numinous has become more insistent means I can't deny the experiences I had today. A poem by Jane Hirshfield says more clearly what I am struggling towards.

Three Times My Life Has Opened

Three times my life has opened.
Once, into darkness and rain.
Once, into what the body carries at all times within it and starts
    to remember each time it enters the act of love.

Once, to the fire that holds all.
These three were not different.
You will recognize what I am saying or you will not.
But outside my window all day a maple has stepped from her leaves
     like a woman in love with winter, dropping   the colored silks.
Neither are we different in what we know.
There is a door. It opens. Then it is closed. But a slip of light
     stays, like a scrap of unreadable paper left on the floor,
     or the one red leaf the snow releases in March.

It seems that today, for an hour or two, the doors of perception were open
and I saw what was beyond. This opening was a gift, or maybe the pay-
off from walking so many miles and, maybe it can all be explained by my
being tired and in an altered state. Whatever the reason, the only
response I have to such a gift is gratitude.

Of course, sensations like this can't last forever, and thank goodness.
Such a heightened state would be unbearable for any length of time, and
is maybe a precursor to psychosis or worse. As the main road and
buildings draw nearer, and it's them doing the drawing, as it still doesn't
feel like me walking towards them, my legs grow heavy and the dull ache
of PMT reminds me that I am, after all, embodied. The world is concrete
again, literally, under my boots and I'm hungry.

There's a restaurant standing alone at the roadside with long tables in a
shady courtyard, unlikely and inviting, but in keeping with the strange
wonder of the morning. I feel strange as I sit down, as if something has
profoundly shifted in the way it did over twenty years ago in Istanbul
when the presence of God made itself undeniably visible in the form of
light in a chapel. I'm stunned, unsure what to make of it all.

Today, corroboration comes from Marie Jose, a petite French woman
I'd met in the hostel in Ambasmestas two days ago. She's in her sixties and
is walking doggedly and seriously and has a luminous air about her. I
now wonder whether she's a nun. She comes into the restaurant a few
minutes after me and plonks herself down opposite. Her eyes are shining
and her long grey hair is escaping in little strands from her neat bun and
she says, 'C'est comme si les anges nous avaient portées jusqu'ici'. She looks
at me in a gently challenging way, and I nod. She holds my gaze, as if
wanting to check I've really heard what she's said and something passes

between us. I'm thinking it wasn't as if there were angels, there really had been angels. She nods and smiles and moves away to put her feet up at another table. From her expression, I suspect she read my thoughts and agreed.

It's not every day angels carry you along, so it feels like cause for celebration. I order an ice cold beer to go with croquettes and a salad. The terrace is in an idyllic spot, warm with a breeze blowing through the courtyard and a quiet murmur of lunching pilgrims. Hamish and Clive, my familiars, are here of course, finishing their lunch. It seems that ever since our farewells several days ago, we are fated to encounter each other over and over. I've started thinking they're my *animus* embodied, both attractive men, with their established businesses and marriages, their second homes in France, confidence and physicality, that is, everything I'm not. One is more expansive and vulnerable, the other quieter and self-contained. They are also my 'roads not taken' – an appropriate *camino* metaphor, in terms of relationships. They are kind of men I imagine many women would aspire to marry, capable, easy company, intelligent, friendly, far better husband material than my own choice of a controversial figure twenty eight years my senior, part of the succession of artist, actor, writer, artist, writer, actor who've comprised my stop-start romantic history. I'm always pleased to see them, and I'm pleased to know that they both have wives waiting at home, so that I can safely ask myself why I've been incapable of developing a nice, normal relationship, with a nice, normal man.

And then my mood changes or rather, is changed for me. My German tormentor of last night arrives with his son. They sit down opposite me at the same table, filling the space with their large bodies and in response, my mind fills with pompous, judgemental thoughts. One inner voice says that really, someone who snores so loudly should have to stay in hotels, and not be allowed in dormitories, another righteously adds that if he didn't drink so much beer and lost some weight, he wouldn't make such a racket when he slept. Yet another voice complains that he is, simply by being here, in front of me now, spoiling my lunchtime idyll by making me anxious as to how I'm going to ensure I don't sleep anywhere near him tonight.

With an act of mental somersaulting, and to shut these thoughts up, I decide to be sociable and ask them how they are. The father speaks no

English but his son is sweet and serious and tells me he's a PhD student in some aspect of physics I've forgotten. His father is finding the walk hard, but it's important for them to spend time together and it's a special time for them. I sense a loss of some kind. Perhaps the mother is no longer around. After ten minutes of chatting about this and that, the son earnestly composing perfect formal sentences and his father gazing in rapt admiration at his fluency in English, my rancour has evaporated. I no longer hate my torturer and am touched by his son's tenderness as he orders more food for his father, finds out for him where the toilet is, passes him a napkin before being asked. Again, I feel a pang for an intimacy I don't have and realise the big man reminds me of my own large-framed, heavy father who died younger than I am now. I remember him saying to a stranger, when I was behaving in a particularly girly way, he wished he'd had 'a couple of lusty boys' instead of two daughters. These German men could be the ghosts of my dead father and the phantom son he never had, enjoying their beer in the sunshine.

Suddenly, the field of stars takes on another dimension. The field is my life, especially given my name, inherited from my father. 'Plough the field that is given to you' was an injunction from the Czech composer Janácek, you sometimes shared with students. When we got together, the phrase became sexually loaded with my name being Field. !!!!! as your letters would say. And here in this field of my walk, are not only those beloved dead I've known well, in the form of large, identifiable stars, but also, in a Milky Way of little pricks of stardust, sprinkled over the firmament, are my unborn brothers and all my own unconceived children. I suddenly feel full of mad love for this pair of strangers.

This is what PMT is like, hatred turning to love, or compassion to fury in a fraction of a second. My sudden change of heart is probably reflected in my daffy smile. In any case, the two men retreat slightly from the potty-looking Englishwoman and talk about getting on with the afternoon's walking. I decided to give them some space and briskly set off ahead of them.

Beer's not a good idea at lunch time and soon I'm slowing down. I pass a bleak-looking municipal hostel on a traffic island, then carry on another couple of miles to a purpose-built low-lying building with a big front lawn, belonging more to American suburbia than peasant Galicia. It's the wrong side of the town I hoped to reach today, but it's another gift, the kind of hostel I haven't seen before and didn't expect on the *camino*. The ranch style bungalow smells of new wood and incense and has half a dozen small dormitories with just eight beds in each, a couple of private rooms with double beds and modern, pristine bathrooms. Even less probable, the proprietor's hippy brother is visiting and offering reiki to tired pilgrims. I check in, then relax, mindlessly swinging in a chair on the lawn.

A pilgrim's dinner is served in a high-ceilinged room straight from an interior design magazine, with generous sofas, interesting paintings and a library of books on the *camino*. I'm achy, edgy and premenstrual and thankful for this calm, homely atmosphere. It's just what I need. If I had to have another sleepless night in a huge communal dormitory, padding through puddles of pee around grotty toilets and queueing for a shower clogged with the hair of strangers, the fuzzy cloud of love I acquired today on the walk would evaporate instantly. I would have become a murderous, screaming banshee, unaccountable for my actions but here, the tranquility is impossible to resist.

Twelve of us sit round a big wooden table and eat lentil soup, buttery tortilla (the establishment is vegetarian), with red wine and fruit. The German men are here and, thank you God, sleeping in a room far from mine. Two of the young Spaniards from Villafranca, days before, sit either side of me and are flirty and fun. There's an attractive Dutch woman desperate to shed another German man who's been trying to pick her up for days. He gazes moonily across at her throughout the meal. And there's an earnest, elderly couple from Vancouver, who look more like gender-ambiguous twins than husband and wife in their identical beige trousers and shirts. Aging often seems to lead to couples growing physically alike, older women looking more masculine and men becoming facially like their mothers. Perhaps it's a version of people looking like their dogs but whether it's to do with the kinds of choices we make subliminally, is, like the Holy Trinity, a mystery.

Salva's hands hover over me as I lay on his couch. He closes his eyes as he moves them around, magically creating little pools of heat or coolness in my aching body. I've no idea how long the treatment goes on for as he has to shake me awake at the end. I stumble back to my bed where I sleep a long deep dreamless sleep in a bunk that doesn't move.

Chapter Eight

After apple picking

I'm slow starting today. I've missed the dawn and instead have a daylight breakfast in a bar in the grotty outskirts of Sarria, with the young Spaniards from last night, David and Manuel. They are as much interested in my Englishness as me and it turns out Manuel teaches English in a Madrid school and David worked for a year in Colchester, as a pharmacist, and developed a taste for Tesco's donuts. I can't believe we then, in the suburbs of Sarria, deep into the *camino*, have a discussion about the shelf-life and value for money of Tesco's donuts.

They're ten, or maybe even twenty, years younger than me, and gallant and gentlemanly. They constantly express concern, pulling back the bar stool for me to clamber up, interpreting for the waiter when I don't need them to, lifting my pack, offering to pay for my coffee. Standing either side of me at the bar, they ask all kinds of questions about my life, write down their email addresses and don't permit me the nun-like anonymity I've cultivated these post-marriage years. It's clear their Spanish chivalry is responding to me as a woman, something I find unfamiliar and disorienting. My guard is down and I've lowered my standards, in the literal, battlefield meaning of the phrase. Somehow, in surrendering to the experiences of yesterday, I'm different, less defended.

It's the day of the month when I usually retreat from the world or else, with my grumpy short fuse, make the world wish I had. I manage to do that for an hour or so in Sarria, by saying farewell to David and Manuel and hanging around waiting for the Post Office to open. I'm relieved to box up my camera and post it home to Cornwall.

Then I potter around the touristy town centre and have a hot chocolate, surplus to requirements when I've not long had breakfast, and a sugary indulgence when I've walked only a few miles. The hot chocolate is a mini-rebellion but against no identifiable oppressor, other than my puritanical conscience. If I was walking as part of a couple, this dilly-dallying might have led to an argument, some sulking and my partner going on ahead in annoyance. Part of me would like the release of tension that can come from a bit of meaningless bickering.

I waste yet more time chatting with the Vancouver couple from last night's hostel, and discover, improbably, that I once worked with her brother. The world seems to shrink again, as it does more and more as the years pass, with seemingly unrelated incidents and acquaintances making links. And I wander around Sarria a bit more, wanting to hide from the world with my aching, bleeding body.

Eventually, I muster the energy to leave the town behind, walk a bit faster and enjoy the brightening day now the morning chill has dissipated. It's clear that Santiago is getting closer or rather, more pilgrims are getting closer to Santiago. Sarria is the starting point for the minimum 100km walk that qualifies for the *compostela* certifying the completion of a pilgrimage to Santiago. The centre is pretty and well-kept, full of hotels and gift shops, catering for the steady stream of tourists who come to look at its ancient walls and cobbled streets. The road out of town goes through orchards and the last of the apples hang like little green planets in the bright light. Windfalls give off a whiff of fermentation in the warmth of the sunny day. Chestnut and oak trees are just at the point of turning from green to brown, and there's a steady ebb and flow of new and familiar faces, as well as longish periods of being on my own in the full, sunny silence.

I walk a while with Carolina, the Dutchwoman who's managed to shed her admirer of last night. Later, I'm alongside a refreshingly negative German woman who describes various aspects of the *camino* experience – such as rain, dormitories, boots, food, mountains, towns, villages and shared bathrooms – as either 'shit' or 'total shit'. Predictably, when I mention Cornwall, Rosamund Pilcher comes into the conversation. The German woman mellows and tells me that no matter how 'shit' or 'total shit' life is, once the TV adaptations of her novels are broadcast every Sunday evening, all is well in the world. The eternal serenity of tea being served by a uniformed butler on the manicured lawns of a clifftop house, is, it seems, as reliably comforting as liturgy or kissing relics in a church.

Later, alone, I pass a man with a beard down to his waist coming towards me, leading a laden donkey and muttering to himself. Poor donkey. Poor man. Surprisingly, I've seen few people who, at least externally, seem crazy and, thankfully, no other beasts of burden, apart from a horse tied up on the first night. It isn't clear what nationality the man is, how or whether he can be helped, or by whom. Later that evening, everyone asks each other, 'Did you see that man with the donkey?' as if it's a test of some kind we've all failed.

Last night I dreamed of Harry. He wants me to keep three boxes of something mysterious, cool. In my dream, there are theatre rehearsals at the Eden Project and I am looking after a woman with dementia. She's quiet but I take her into a hospital ward of people who are raving, through a door which says 'Not For Fat Women'. This dream is just a memory, but then so is the man with the donkey, the apples and the ancient walls of Sarria. These memories are slotted inside each other, a dream inside a memory, that at this distance, might as well be a dream. These dreams, memories, hallucinations, fantasies, altered states are like the Russian matryoshka dolls, with only the outer one visible, as my external self in the world as she is now, hiding increasingly small versions of myself, including the one keeping three boxes of something mysterious, cool.

The little restaurant, just before Ferreiros, where I stop for lunch, could be the house Hansel and Gretel found in the woods, all carvings and lace tablecloths. My diary only records, as it does with monotonous regularity, exactly what I ate and how much it cost. So I know I had *empanada*, a kind of Hispanic Cornish pasty, salad and juice, and paid 5.50 euros, but to be honest, I can't be entirely sure about the lace tablecloths.

There's a large party sitting outside, lunching together at a circular table. They seem to be part of an organised tour group that's busy looking at each other, rather than outwards at the environment or into their own hearts. I enjoy all the camaraderie and banter in the evenings at the pilgrim's dinners, but during the day, I'm happier to go inside the little wooden building and share my table with another solitary pilgrim.

But am I inventing the table linen? Am I conflating this little place with the restaurant we ate in at Yasnaya Polyana in 2002, which was also a small wooden structure in the woods? Are there really carvings?

Perhaps if I was in a group, more than one of us would notice the pretty tablecloths, and I would be more certain. Someone might comment that carvings remind him of those he's seen in Soviet Georgia, and then I'd have confirmation that I'm in the realm of memory, not dream. Is it necessary to write the facts, or is it enough as Philip Roth allegedly suggested, to 'imagine the facts'. The fact that he calls his 1989 autobiography 'The Facts' seems like provocation although, of course, that is a fact, because he definitely did it.

The early meanings of the word 'fact', some now considered archaic, are all to do with actions and deeds, rather than pieces of information that are 'true'. Yes, I sat down in a little restaurant and ate *empanada*, I'm sure about that. And I sat opposite a man who was walking on his own, and have an impression of greyness but no other memory of him. On reflection, though, the lace tablecloths seem unlikely, even if, as I write this several months later, I'm sure I remember them clearly.

Buried in those Russian-doll recollections is a persistent association of empanadas with a trip to Bolivia in 1984 on the first year of Operation Raleigh. In the mock-Spanish we developed, we called *empanadas*, 'them bananas'. Charlie, Dougie and Robin, people I haven't thought of for years, suddenly become real and vivid in my memory and 'them bananas' makes smile even though I haven't thought of them for a quarter of a century. Again the pilgrimage becomes life in microcosm. Those three men, one of whom saved my life, are people I chatted with on a section of the path of my life, and have never seen again. They are conjured by a single word, *empanadas*, which jumps across decades and continents. William James in his 'Talks To Teachers' in 1899, is on to something when he writes about memory,

> … that an impression will vibrate throughout the brain, and send waves into other parts of it. In cases of this sort, although the immediate impression may fade out quickly, it does modify the cerebral mass; for the paths it makes there may remain, and become so many avenues through which the impression may be reproduced if they ever get excited again …

The little wooden hut is enough to shake the 'gelatinous substance' of my brain and send me walking along the familiar pathways that include lace tablecloths and you, because little wooden huts remind me of Russia. I lived there for over three years before I met you, but subsequently my

Russia has merged with the version that's your Russia and our Russia, because it was connections with that country that drew us together at the beginning of our relationship. To use the language of William James, you've shaken the jelly of my brain so thoroughly, that most of its paths and avenues, Soviet-style, are named after you. And many of the central squares of my memory have you standing in them on a plinth, holding open your coat and pointing to Moscow. My continuing to live in Cornwall since our break-up means the avenues of my cerebral mass are forever being re-excited by impressions of our past. The memories stampede up and down with such force that the flagstones, kerbs and cobbles are worn down by the simple passing there.

Just as way leads on to way, the image of the worn path takes me back to a time just after Christmas, before we married when I thought, I must, once and for all, put an end to our affair and make a clean break for the New Year. I called to tell you. You knew I meant it and panicked. Your first response was a fax, telling me you'd like me to have your large collection of books about Russia, the library you'd acquired when researching the vast and scholarly biography that took several years and was the reason, initially, we saw each other again. I was puzzled until I realised the fax was a coded suicide note. You always told me that in spite of some serious depressions, you'd never seriously thought of 'visiting Yelabuga', the Tatar city where Marina Tsvetaeva took her own life in 1941. Suddenly, uncharacteristically, it seemed you were planning on travelling east. There was then a great flurry of phone calls, criss-crossing via your children, who called me in my little Chester two-up two-down where I was resolving to break free, start again, put you behind me.

But, just as you later insisted on telephoning me every day in Pakistan, you were determined not to let me go. That evening, you made a seemingly impossible, long, expensive journey through holiday engineering works, all the way from Truro to Chester, changing at Birmingham New Street and goodness knows where else, and emerged on the station platform in your familiar camel coat and rabbit fur hat. Of course I was there to meet you. In those days, there were still smoking compartments on the trains. I wonder now if we would have gone our separate ways much sooner if the smoking ban had come in earlier. Certainly those train journeys would have been less tolerable for you.

It became as clear to me as it already was to you, that we couldn't part, at least not yet, that we still had a journey to make together. One of the things we did during those dark in-between Christmas and New Year days, was to drive out to the Peak District and walk up the 1600 feet or so of Mam Tor, the 'Heights of the Mother', not far from the Hope Valley.

There was a bitter wind and you hated walking so, looking back, the whole outing was improbable. The paths up the iconic hill are deep, well-worn by the boots of the quarter of a million or so walkers who come every year. The climb came unexpectedly easily to you, like a stroll down memory lane, and you were rosy-cheeked and exhilarated when got back in the car. Some memory lanes have been walked so often, they've become deep channels in the landscape with sides so high, it's impossible to see over. Like parts of the *camino* or the path up Mam Tor, they are worn and need officials with fence posts and wire to come and redirect the walkers, encouraging them to take a new route, with fresh views, one less destructive to the environment.

After the Hansel and Gretel cafe of faulty memories, the *camino* moves in and out of hamlets, along lanes and farm tracks, all easy, relaxed walking, except I'm anxious about my period which is at its heaviest point. Among my peri-menopausal friends, we sometimes talk about the changes that we're experiencing in our menstruation, the possibility of what's called, not euphemistically, 'flooding'. I first heard the term when I was a college lecturer in my early twenties, when my periods could be achy and painful, but didn't involve much bleeding. Two mature students collared me after their evening class, worried about their forthcoming A'Level exam which, for both of them, would coincide with the middle of their periods. Would they be able to go out to the loo? What if the invigilator suspected them of writing notes on the inside of boxes of tampons or sanitary towels? What if they 'flooded' whilst getting carried away writing their answers? I didn't know what they were talking about.

Throughout my twenties and most of my thirties, I intermittently took the pill. It's a form of chemical castration and I felt less sexual and less alive generally whilst taking it. When I was twenty three, I risked coming off it, thinking it would be a while before my fertility came back, but immediately conceived with my steady boyfriend of the time. I was in my first job, had just stretched myself financially buying a tiny terraced house in Chester and made the mistake of confiding in my boss. He was head of the psychology department at the college and was instrumental in getting me a full-time permanent lecturer post in spite of my youth and inexperience. He was also the college's Randy Andy who made a speciality of counselling and then bedding young art students, at a time when such behaviour was just how things were and no one thought to challenge him. He assumed, of course I'd want a termination, as did the Pregnancy Advisory Service, and I assumed I did too, although most of the time I was too nauseous to think clearly.

To have a child would mean taking a road leading into a part of the woods full of overhanging branches and overgrown with brambles, whereas I was well on my way to a dappled career path and the sunny clearings of financial stability. It was interesting to be pregnant, to be in such an altered state but I couldn't imagine parenthood and had no role models to draw on. The first, very early sign that suggested I wasn't quite myself, was being unable to eat anything that had been anywhere near a microwave. In addition, I was bloated, spotty, worried and generally felt pretty rough.

After the abortion, people complemented me on how well I looked, my breasts were no longer tender and swollen and life was simple again. But in reality, my boyfriend and I were broken-hearted. I read a Women's Press book of first person accounts of abortions over and over again trying to locate my own experience in those of others. Memories of the clinic are mixed up with images from the television which was on in the waiting room, screening the memorial service for the 193 passengers who'd died in the Herald of Free Enterprise ferry disaster. I'd only a few years previously been working as an au pair in Ostend and had travelled home to Kent on those ferries regularly. So many deaths, so much sadness, and me sitting in a waiting room in a clinic specifically set up to destroy another life. The anaesthetist had a kind face and a warm voice and on his instruction, I began to count to ten, sinking into oblivion around five. I woke up in a bed next to that of a girl who was probably only about twelve years old, whose mother and sister sat either side of her, reminiscing about their own abortions.

Liverpool was bright and sunny the next day and as I queued outside the clinic for a bus back to the station, a couple of tough-looking local women who'd also had the 'procedure' told me, as so many others would, that I looked like a weight had lifted.

I went straight back to work. A month or so later, my boss invited me to his bungalow, a mass of botched DIY, where he made me a curry, then seduced me on the carpet of his living room, in front of a video of 'The Life of Brian', his favourite film. My boyfriend's mum, a feminist, told me she was all in favour of a woman's right to choose, but had felt differently when it was her own grandchild. A few months later, my boyfriend and I went on holiday to North Wales, and following a suggestion from a drama therapist, I wanted to say a proper farewell to the unborn child and took a bunch of roses to the end of the Lleyn peninsula. I later wrote a poem that's the first in a series of poems featuring lost children and prefigures this pilgrimage over twenty years later.

Bardsey Island

On Bardsey Island, I built a bivvy
from my baby's bones
and let the white wind whisper to me
through its gap-toothed walls

My baby's ear was a shell
washed up onto the shore
telling me *hey diddle diddle* as the sea
chuckles the pebbles around my feet

On Bardsey Island I gathered the souls
of the good and the bad and the damned
and played them face-down like patience
to trick the world into making her whole

A fat red heart came rolling towards me
surprised, like an adder in the bracken
and her smiles bounced through the clover to
the chink of spades in the flinty graves

From Bardsey Island, to make it all come right,
I set sail in a coracle to Cornwall
went spinning with the flying fish
then walked the dusty road alone to Rome

Countries popped up, colourful as picture books
my knees bled on the stairs to Roquemadour
but still, *fee fo fie fum*, my Bardsey baby is no more.
The angels have won and taken her home.

Every period is a missed potential pregancy, a letting-go of possibility.
The average woman will have five hundred periods in her lifetime, five
hundred opportunities to mourn a child who won't be born. And even
those who have children are haunted by ghosts of these unconceived
offspring. In my own circle, women with one child feel guilty that their son
or daughter has no siblings, I know a mother of four sons who yearns for a
daughter with whom to share the feminine aspects of life, another with two
beautiful daughters, tells me the family dog is a substitute for the son they
never had. A friend is the youngest of six girls and considers herself the
final disappointment, the point when her parents stopped trying.

When my fortieth birthday was coming up over the horizon like a
huge ticking time bomb of a sun, I became obsessed with trying to get
pregnant by you. Not unreasonably for someone well into his sixties,
with his own children pushing forty, you weren't enthusiastic. You told
me you'd go along with it but I couldn't expect you to be a hands-on
father. I had no illusions, and knew any baby we had would be totally my
responsibility. I kept little charts by the bed, plotted my temperature on
graphs and spent hours on internet sites where women discussed fertility.
Still, my periods came as predictably as the moon, waking me with a
familiar dull ache on Day 28. I went to the GP and had my hormones
tested, they were fine. Did I put you through the indignity of having your
sperm count assessed? I do remember joking about them coughing and
wheezing in their microscopic millions.

The next step was an ultrasound at the local private hospital where
everything happened with no waiting whatsoever, and I paid a substantial bill before leaving. A doctor, with the help of an alarming-looking
dildo wired up to a bank of machines going beep, was able to show me
my own uterus and ovaries which looked, even on the grainy, monochrome monitor, as bewitching as a Georgia O'Keefe painting. They, too,
were fine. The next investigation would be the injection of some kind of
luminous dye to see whether my tubes were open. Somehow, I never got
round to booking the appointment.

The sense of urgency passed, but not before I experienced such overwhelming baby-hunger, I tried to conceive with someone else. Given your own infidelities, I felt it would be something you'd understand, the biological imperative driving a human being to extreme behaviour, but you were furious in a way I hadn't seen before. I don't think it was sexual jealousy but more the atavistic fear of a cuckoo in the nest. It seemed inconsistent when there are examples of dubious paternity combined with loving parenting in your own circle of friends. My only defence, my lord, is diminished responsibility, being on a roller coaster of hormones, seeing that wretched sun moving inexorably through my one day of fertile womanhood, getting ever lower as summer yields to autumn.

Since I've been celibate these past five years, I've felt calmer as if my body has forgotten what all that swelling and bleeding is about. I've lost touch with aspects of my womanhood. Sometimes, I see my breasts in the bathroom mirror, and I'm surprised and think, what on earth are they for? Instead of a warm, responsive human body, I'm more like a satellite orbiting the moon as she trails through the months, aware that things are subtly changing and at some point, not too distant, we'll decouple. The moon will carry on doing her thing and I'll become increasingly androgynous in my post-menopausal guise.

But it hasn't happened yet, and mid-afternoon, I'm uncomfortable. It's been a couple of hours since lunchtime and I've been walking steadily, something which is both relaxing for the pain but which increases the menstrual flow. I have a horrible feeling I might be flooding. There are no towns or large villages on the route for at least another ten kilometres. I start to panic, wondering what I can possibly do. The path isn't crowded by any means, but there are always other pilgrims popping up behind me or else I'm catching up with them, and there's no privacy behind hedges or gates. I think of the poor bleeding woman of the gospels, unclean for twelve whole years and healed in an instant by touching Christ's robe. She was boldly transgressive by doing so. Her touch would make Him ritually unclean, as it would all the others she brushed up against in the crowd. Just as Christ cured her in a flash, modern medicine offers a lifeline to all women who struggle with their periods, the possibility of an instant cure by way of a hysterectomy. Of those I know who've taken that option, some say they've never felt better, at last they are free to be themselves. whilst others feel, that word again, castrated and mourn the loss of what they see as an integral part of themselves.

At one point, I pass a woman standing in the yard of a run-down farm. I can see a house beyond the barns. It looks uninviting and unhygienic, but I'm desperate and ask her whether she has access to a toilet. I try to look needy and trustworthy and will her to invite me into her home. Instead she tells me there's one not far off, a few hundred metres at most. In the language of my young friends, I so totally don't believe her. We are deep in rural Galicia and the nearest village is another ten kilometres away. She insists, then shoos me away with her rake so I have no choice but to carry on, feeling my life's blood draining away between my legs. This is another point on the walk I want to cry, not with those tears of devotion so frequently offered by Margery Kempe, but with shame and frustration.

But, like a mirage, just off the little path with its hedgerows and brambles, its nothing-but-the-countryside-ness, there's a brand new *albergue*, so new it isn't listed in my little guide. It's not just any kind of *albergue*, but a boutique affair with a brightly coloured main building, a walled garden and, most incongruous of all, a bar complex, painted in purple and mauve with a variety of black and chrome chairs around glass tables. It looks more in keeping with a Caribbean island resort, than the muddy Galician countryside. It has the same miraculous quality as a shimmering oasis in the desert. The toilets are brand new and spotless, with hot and cold water, paper towels, hand-driers and a groovy mirror for brushing hair and applying lipstick, everything one could possibly wish for and, as the song goes, just when I needed it most.

Once I've sorted myself out, relieved at having maintained the Western illusion that women don't menstruate, something puzzling to women in developing countries who don't understand our invisible periods, I sit for some time in the cafe and celebrate with a mid-afternoon glass of Rioja, browsing the glossy magazines that litter the bar area.

I can only think that the place is newly built in anticipation of the increased numbers of pilgrims expected next year, a Jubilee Year when the Feast of St James falls on a Sunday. For Roman Catholics especially, a pilgrimage made in a Jubilee Year has special significance. In this ordinary year, in scruffy rural Galicia, the complex is empty and seems bizarre, but beautifully so.

The route on to Portomarín is pleasant, zig-zagging around fields where peasant farmers go about their business, slow and relaxed in their movements, occasionally raising a hand in greeting and calling 'Buen Camino' to a passing pilgrim. As I near the city, a couple come towards me, driving their cows home, beating them along with knobbly sticks. They've solved the problem of any of the animals wandering off by hobbling them, that is tying one of their rear legs up in a bent position so that all of the dozen creatures are in effect three-legged and crippled, thrown off balance and struggling and stumbling down the bumpy track. It's a miserable picture.

Many cultures have shamanic beliefs about animals, including theories of how their auras can communicate with us. Such ideas are taken seriously by Western nature writers such as Barry Lopez and Jim Perrin. The aura around these cows encompasses the closed-faced couple driving them along, and it's dank, sad and heavy, the aura of trapped creatures everywhere, whether in farms, on hospital wards, in prisons, loveless marriages or by poverty or depression. Please, I want to say to the couple, let them walk naturally and if one should hive off and over the hills, let her go. An animal making its escape, whether a pig running from the slaughterhouse, the elephant packing her trunk or the legendary cat and dog on their incredible journey, is a potent archetype in our culture and yet we persist in trapping ourselves and others.

Freedom too has an aura, the bright one of a hare seen in the distance, high on its hind legs in a sunlit field, the diamond one of a swan gliding in to land on a lake or a kingfisher speeding up a river. On this walk, there's a collective aura, of 'pilgrimage', I suppose, one that is luminous and free and also cohesive like a mountain stream or a rainbow, many things and one thing all at the same time. It's only by walking through its opposite, hanging like a cloud around the wilfully crippled cows, that I become aware of the beauty of the pilgrim aura.

Portomarín is a strange place. The approach is across a vast valley with a small river in the middle, which someone tells me is actually a reservoir, where the water has run low. The empty valley has an apocalyptic quality. There's a large slipway in the distance hovering in empty space, the water having receded hundreds of metres from the shore. It's hard to get a sense of perspective. A scrap of red plastic that seems not far away, turns out to be a distant cyclist in brightly coloured clothes, pedalling towards me along the wide bank.

I intended to treat myself tonight to a hotel. It's yet another freedom I enjoy, not just to walk, but, within reason, to spend what I like on food and accommodation. The town is marooned high above the river-reservoir and incongruously small compared to the vast valley beneath, and its few *pensiones* aren't appealing. Instead, I check into a shiny modern hostel that looks like a hospital, all white tiles, big windows and well-mopped floors. It has one single, vast dormitory overlooking the river valley with so many identical bunks, the effect is like an enormous carpark where it's easy to lose a vehicle in the repeating expanse of similar objects. But it's not busy and there's a generous amount of space around each bunk and, an unexpected bonus, large single-sex bathrooms with rows of steaming power showers.

The main square of the town is dominated by a church dedicated to St Nicholas and built between the twelfth and thirteenth century. I join Hamish and Clive who've just had supper in a restaurant in one of the covered arcades around the square. We watch coachloads of tourists stream out of their vehicles, go into the church briefly and then load up again and drive away. I later read that the church, like most of the old buildings in the town, was moved stone by stone to its place on the hill when the original village was flooded in order to build a dam. The same article tells me, 'Portomarín is obliged passage for pilgrims in their way to Santiago de Compostela and as a village at a reservoir the eel it is really tasty!'. The Pilgrim Menu at the restaurant doesn't include eel and I'm not very hungry so I simply order a glass of wine and accept one of Clive's mini Monte Christo cigars, enjoying the buzz and rich flavour. On my way back to the hostel, I have an appetite after all, so pop into the super-market for some sardines and pasta which I cook up in the big modern kitchen where no one appears to have used any of the utensils, every-thing's so new and shiny.

The idea of the village being rebuilt stone by stone bothers me. Am I in Portomarín or not? It reminds me of a rare psychiatric disorder, Capgras Syndrome, where a person is convinced that a friend or spouse or family member has been replaced by an identical-looking imposter. Any memoir, I suppose, is a kind of Capgras in that the version of you I'm creating detail by detail, although it looks to me exactly like the you I remember, will seem to those who know you, not quite right. In the same way, the light that comes into St Nicholas's Church can't be the same at the top of the hill as it was down in the valley.

Egeria is good at picking up on how buildings and natural features might differ in the fourth century from biblical accounts, but in the fourth century, buildings aren't moved from one place to another. Buildings, like trees, are rooted and integral to their surroundings and simply aren't the same if they are moved. A caravan or tent is a different entity from a house or office block.

Humans and other mobile creatures remain the essentially same, even when, on the surface at least, the cells of the body may have renewed themselves and changed, or they look a bit different out of context . When I see you these days, it's after relatively long intervals and I'm often surprised by how you look, either older or younger, healthier or less so, than I'd expected, but there's no doubting that it's you. When we were married though, I couldn't really have said what you looked like, you were simply familiar and your presence was as much your way of moving through the house, our conversations or the way we touched, as the physical reality of your body. Perhaps these intangible dimensions are part of what makes the *camino* the *camino*, more than just a worn path through a landscape.

St Nicholas, when it was down in the valley, would have been occupied for centuries by a continuous, overlapping series of priests and worshippers, pilgrims and tourists, all lighting candles and saying prayers where candles and prayers had been since the place was built. The rupture of the place being taken apart must have jolted something of the sacred geometry of the original building, so that the prayers rise differently and the candles flicker in a way that's subtly not the same. You move through the same house you've lived in for decades with your fourth wife, but I doubt it's in exactly the same way you did when you and I shared it, or when you were with your second wife.

Every step on the floorboards or the kitchen floor, every word spoken, every kiss exchanged, must at some level leave a trace in the house so, even if we decided to pick up where we left off six years ago, I wouldn't be entirely sure you were really you and might scream that there's an imposter in our bed and demand that someone challenge that man wearing your dressing gown and sitting in your study.

I wonder who I am now, as I slide into my sleeping bag, happy at the space around me in this large airy dormitory. I'm certainly not the weeping woman of Bloomsbury, nor the smiling bride, happy to have her friends around her, nor am I quite the same woman who left Cornwall a week or so before. Like the Church of St Nicholas, I've moved up the hill, and whilst I might seem the same, I know I'm not.

Chapter Nine

More ghosts

I'm well over a day ahead of the schedule I envisaged. I've no need now to hurry, to clock up the miles, to get anywhere in particular. I feel the same sense of space, of time as a gift, that I get when a meeting or arrangement is cancelled at the last minute. Even if there's disappointment, there's a sudden liberation when time that was committed becomes free. What was coloured in with the various hues of socialising or work, is now transparent and once again available.

My days feel more elastic. Instead of setting off before dawn, I'm happy to start with a coffee on the terrace of the Mirador, watching the line of pilgrims trail down through the town and along the distant westerly bank of the river. Eventually I pull on my pack to join them and make my way down the steep streets, back towards the river. There are many more pilgrims than I've seen on previous days. It's the weekend and, inevitably, there are more people walking the closer we get to Santiago.

It starts to drizzle and it's cold, so I rev up my walking speed and find myself easily overtaking the anonymous people ahead of me. With their faces obscured by voluminous waterproofs, they're distinguished only by their different heights and whether or not they're carrying a staff. I'm feeling rested and fit, and am easily covering the miles when suddenly, I tread on a rock-hard windfall apple, no bigger than a walnut. I slide forward Charlie-Chaplin-style, then back, then sideways, then, by frantically windmilling my arms, steady myself and thankfully, don't fall over. I have weak ankles, prone to breaks and sprains. I once spent a miserable six months recovering from an Achilles tendon injury sustained doing nothing more strenuous than skipping through the Gay Gordons. Today, miraculously, I've only very mildly pulled my left ankle and the discomfort is easily dissipated by continuing to walk.

But I'm chastened. The balloon of my pride in speeding along, feeling smug and inviolable, has been well and truly pricked. I'm aware, again, of how vulnerable a body is, how my well-being and happiness could have gone in an instant if I'd tumbled over that tiny little apple and heard the sadly familiar crack of a bone snapping in my ankle. How all the joy of the last week and the anticipation of the final part of the walk, could be wiped out with the inconvenience of a casualty department, plaster casts and awkward crutches.

I carry on in a more measured way, focusing on my breathing, feeling grateful for my luck and looking forward to breakfast in the next village. The one cafe in Ganzar is packed to the gills. The rain is steady now and everyone has crowded into the steamed-up space, jostling for plastic chairs and space at the tables. I'm transported to similar places on wet walks in the Lakes or Snowdonia There's the same smell of wet clothes and boots even if the hubbub has different, more international rhythm. I have a juice, a roll and another coffee and talk to three ladies from Quebec who are formal and distantly polite.

After the cafe, the pilgrims spread out and the road gives way to a track through fragrant woodland. I slow down and enjoy the peace and solitude, the gentle rain and simple fact I'm still walking, that the malevolent apple hasn't claimed me as its prey. The track crosses shady lanes, giving glimpses of pretty farmhouses and the going is easy. The next few hours pass in a blur, there's a just a sense of walking, sometimes climbing slightly, mostly through conifers, on a bed of last year's shedded needles, my mind doing its own thing, not agitating but leaving me with a sense of peace.

There's a pretty roadside restaurant on one of the little lanes and I stop for lunch of a *Caldo Gallego*, the local bean and cabbage-filled soup. Although still rainy, it's now warm so I sit outside on the veranda. At first I'm alone, then a Canadian father and son roll up and ask if they can join me. I feel I've known them all my life. Bill is quick and talkative, full of gentle wise-cracks and Fergus, in his early twenties, is relaxed and witty too, quick to pick up the baton of his dad's jokes. They're an attractive pair, open and eager to be friendly. I recommend the soup, which they order, and then they also ask for a bottle of red wine. My resolve dissolves in an instant. I join them in a glass, then two, and soon we're laughing and enjoying each other's company even more.

They greet an American woman who is walking alone. She too sits down with us and I learn they met some time ago, all of them having come the whole way from St-Jean-Pied-de-Port. There's a shared history which I'm not part of, but I feel sure that this trio are my friends already. Mandy is feisty and funny too.

Eventually, we get up to leave. Bill is suffering with his feet and walks gingerly, so I go on ahead, not fast, not slow, simply letting the Way walk me at whatever pace it chooses.

I catch up with an Australian woman who is limping, but somehow manages to keep up a brisk, if jerky, pace. She's not carrying anything at all which gives her a curiously naked appearance amongst the laden pilgrims, as if she's a tortoise without a shell. She gives me the low-down on how she and her husband have 'cracked' the *camino*. They spent just one night in an *albergue* and decided, no way, it was going to be hotels from now on. Then they had just one day carrying their back packs and decided, no way, from now on, they'd use a baggage service to carry their luggage on to their next night's destination. In spite of her painful feet, Linda insists she's having a great time, her only gripe being the way her husband Paul keeps on striding out ahead of her. In the annoying way of fast walkers, he waits for her to catch up at a cafe or restaurant but then, as soon as she arrives, is agitating to get going. Paul and Linda are totally focused on getting to Santiago as quickly and comfortably as possible so that they can carry on with their complicated tour around Europe with several countries squeezed into their brief annual leave. I too, leave Linda behind and walk on ahead.

You and I were often out of synch during our courtship, living far apart. I wasn't just living in Chester, the Midlands or London, but later went as far as I could go, to Pakistan. We managed to meet many times during those years. I made a couple of trips to Cornwall and joined you when you were in London. You valiantly took the train to came further up-country to meet me. We had a couple of holidays and went twice to Russia and Martinique on research trips. I came with you to Calgary where you had a residency and we were both invited to Georgia in 1997, when a hiatus in the various civil wars gave someone the idea of holding a theatre festival at a time when Tbilisi had little electricity or running water.

The glue that held us together during those years when we saw each other intermittently, was that on the envelopes of our vast correspondence. We wrote to each other several times a week, sometimes more than once a day, a mixture of traditional letters, typed and manuscript, cards and faxes. You would often, too, send flowers and once a cassette tape of you reading your favourite poems interspersed with recordings of songs from shows, during which I could hear you padding around your study, lighting a cigarette. Email was a new invention and neither of us had it then and texts were unheard of, so it was pen on paper, or else something typed and scribbled on. I think you disposed of my letters as they arrived, but I kept a stash of yours, eventually filling three large carrier bags.

I was constantly on the move and aware that these letters were treasure of a kind, a correspondence that went right up to the wire of the electronic revolution. We agreed I'd give them to the man who dealt with the manuscripts of your early books, who would keep them safe. When, a decade later, you sent me an email to say you'd had remarried because, apparently, immigration regulations for your girlfriend were making things impossible, I was shocked as if I'd been hit on the head and concussed.

I left my desk in the farmhouse and walked several miles along the deep moorland lanes, with no idea where I was headed, in an attempt to gather my thoughts. Even though I knew you liked being married and had been, during your whole adult life, usually married with the next wife lined up, I was still taken by surprise at the suddenness. Your email was a punctuation point, an unequivocal ending and the news felt like that of a death and funeral rolled into one.

One of my first thoughts was that I'd like to have your letters back. I called the dealer in his smart London premises, coincidentally just opposite my friend's Bloomsbury flat. Of course, he said smoothly, he had them in a safe in his cellar and would look them out if I dropped by, which a few weeks later, I did. He sent his assistant down to fetch them and seemed genuinely nonplussed when the younger man came back upstairs empty-handed. He was dressed for a Booker dinner and began plucking at the orchid in his button-hole, before eventually expressing regret at destroying something wonderful. I thought he meant losing my letters, but he meant the flower that he'd absent-mindedly shredded as we talked. A couple of days later, he called me to say that, now, he remembered, you'd been in London on your own and had called in to his shop, in a panic, saying that the letters might be incriminating in some way and you wanted to get rid of them. I imagine you in those narrow streets, stuffing the three big carrier bags into a wheelie bin behind a restaurant, or perhaps taking them back to Jo's and disposing of them in a dustbin in a black bag of household rubbish. I was livid. The letters are mine, even if the content is yours. Unlike email, they are artefacts, with postage stamps and postmarks, dates and places, they are full of life and energy, they are testimonies of love, and they are mine.

There is something potent about letters. That intense correspondence over five years of passionate love letters, was probably one of the last such, now email and texts have taken over. I still write by hand to a few people, but with them, there's a slow ping-pong of waiting for letters, thinking them over and replying at leisure, sometimes weeks or even months later. The idea of scribbling pages once or twice a day, then running to the post box would seem impossibly eccentric now.

Of course, once we married, the impulse to write letters disappeared, but as we were splitting up, you began again, not posting them, but giving them to me by hand or leaving them on my desk or dressing table. The contents alternated between regrets and promises to change your habits, to lengthy explanations as to how I (and your mother) were to blame, that it was we who pushed you into secrecy and affairs. I still have those letters here, all in the same white business envelope, several with 'To Victoria – this is the last letter, I promise' written on the front. I don't want to read them again but nor do I want to throw them away. They, unlike those lost carrier bags of white envelopes, colourful cards and faded faxes, are relics of you that I've kept from our marriage. In medieval times, when pilgrimage and the reverence of relics were at their peak, people were quick to see the value of body parts and objects connected with saints, even before some were canonised. When Thomas Becket was murdered in Canterbury Cathedral, monks were at the ready to collect phials of his blood, knowing that soon it would be immensely valuable. Your letters to me were similarly deserving of care and reverence, and now, through some kind of reformation, I wasn't even aware of, they've gone, scattered like the bones of saints and whatever remains of Christ's umbilicus or the crown of thorns.

Palas de Rei is pretty well shut on a Sunday evening. There's a choice of hostels. A huge super-modern one in a kind of country park on the outskirts of town reminds me too much of a comprehensive school when I pop in for a pee, so I walk on. The first one, in the town itself, is dingy and out of lower bunks so I check into the next one, a privately run *albergue* above a noisy bar, where a mixture of locals and pilgrims are watching a motorcycle rally on multiple TV screens, their heads all cricked upwards at an uncomfortable angle.

Everything about the hostel is makeshift. There's a row of three showers where ill-fitting curtains mean paddling through mini-floods, before intermittent water pressure sends fits and starts of alternately boiling and freezing water over my tired body. Two ancient washing machines screech and thunder through their cycles and the furniture is cheap and rickety. A saving grace, though, is an incongruous single bed lengthways along the window of the dormitory. Whether there's some rule about not obscuring the window with bunks or whether it's simply a bed going spare, I don't know, but claim it with a cry of delight. After the oppressive feeling of someone sleeping above my head, it's a joy to sprawl across a bed and look all the way up to a ceiling. It's almost like being at home where I sleep in the middle of a double bed, enjoying being able to stretch in every direction. For the first time on the *camino*, I can lie on my bed and look out of the first floor window. I can open the window! I'm in hostel-heaven. I express this to a dapper German man, in his mid-twenties, sitting sighing on his bunk. He immediately complains that it ought to be comfortable, it's so expensive. He tells me that, to be frank, he's fed up with the whole *camino* thing.

I'm delighted too when Bill and Fergus arrive and claim their bunks in the same dormitory, but disconcerted by the sight of Bill's infected toe nail. He's been trying, unsuccessfully, to procure antibiotics for days and his complexion has a strange greenish pallor, reminding me of how, pre-Alexander Fleming, people often died of minor infections, not least Rupert Brooke on his way to the Dardenelles, of a simple mosquito bite. Two Swiss women in their sixties sharing an adjacent bunk, are also concerned and take over in an assertive, knowledgable way, applying creams and dressings. Bill jokes and grimaces, pretending that he isn't worried about the state of his foot. The women aren't at all squeamish.

They are cheerful, practical women like those in my family who've become nurses and take no nonsense.

The bar downstairs seems to be the centre of life in the town. I have a beer on the terrace outside with another Canadian couple from Vancouver, then go exploring. It could be Liskeard or Camborne on a Sunday afternoon, everything is closed in the emphatic way that suggests potential customers or visitors are not so much unwelcome, as totally irrelevant. I walk one way round the town centre, peering into tobacconists and chemists shops and then the other, peering into stationers and banks, then, down a side alley, spot the lights of a small restaurant serving a pilgrim's dinner. Most of the pilgrims I've seen in the town are there and I'm pleased I can squeeze onto a table already occupied by Bill, Fergus and Mandy. We have a relaxed evening of easy, joking, serious talk and I sleep well in my wonderful bed designed for solo occupancy.

Chapter Ten

Octopuses and other animals

Days are starting to blur. Instead of a continuous film, panning over mountains, moving into close-ups of interesting faces, impressive long shots of walking pilgrims, all in real time, the journey is becoming a montage of short clips and still shots. Today's early morning is just a snapshot of a length of pavement, covered in white boot-prints as I follow a line of pilgrims past a bakery.

This morning, I see the same man coming towards me, three times. We greet each other each time as if we were meeting for the first time. It's surreal and funny, like the film 'Ground Hog Day'. Walking to Santiago, I pass trees and houses, shops and farms, but only once, except for this polite Frenchman who's coming towards me yet again.

'*Bonjour*,' we say, as if it's normal, except it's not and on the fourth encounter, I ask him what he's doing. The answer's logical, he's the driver for a group and rather than meet everyone at the end of the day, he goes on a few miles, parks, walks back alone along the Way to see how they are doing and then, they all then carry on to the car, when he drives on again. My *camino* is a continuous line. He will have driven the whole way but only have walked half of it, in little sections, each section done twice, this way and that.

My memories of you too are becoming increasingly like snapshots. In fact, lots of them come to mind in the form of actual photographs, especially one of you on Skyros, the second time we went in 1998. You're tanned, handsome, wearing a black t-shirt, eyes creased against the bright sunlight. It was taken by one of your students, a man, and there's a quizzical look on your face as you stare into the lens of his smart SLR.

That connection between the subject and the photographer's Cyclops eye has disappeared now we wave around our digital cameras or mobile phones. You take a good portrait, somehow your intelligence and intensity is written on your face. I've always preferred those pictures of you looking serious, somehow your smile belongs to a different you, a persona or mask that fits you less well.

You weren't interested in taking photos of me, unless I was half-naked. But there's one I treasure from Christmas Day 2001. It was a big family affair with two of your children, two grand-children, your sister and nephew, your daughter's partner, and I seem to remember there were others. You and I were at each end of the long dining room table and you snapped me as I smiled at you. I look sweaty and squiffy, which I was after cooking all morning in the company of a bottle of sherry. I'd made several lists with accurate timings, counting down to lunch time, to keep me on track as I knew I'd be drinking from early on. The Christmas dinner was a triumph of a beautiful free range bird and all the trimmings, cooked to perfection. I'm glowing, holding a champagne glass, the winter light catching my ear-rings and my smile is full of love for you, this strange family I'd become part of, the joy of Christmas, cooking and people happy around a long table.

There are few photographs of us together. I have one from Russia in 1995, just after we'd met, when we'd gone on a research trip to Rostov, looking at the early homes of Solzhenitsyn, for your mammoth biography, that took several years and was an act of homage to Russian literature. I had an elderly friend in Moscow from the time I lived there. Arthur Raffe's private story, although unknown to the world, is as dramatic as Solzhenitsyn's public one, and I wanted you to meet him. When we arrived in Moscow, I heard he was ill in hospital but we had no time then to visit. After our few days in the South, we flew back from Rostov and went straight from the airport by taxi to the hospital, skidding on the vast ring road in a flurry of early snow.

The nurse who met us at the ward entrance was massive, hatchet-faced with a blood-red slash of lipstick against a gulag-grey face and uniform. When I explained who we'd come to see, she replied grimly, *'Arthur umir,'* and seeing my confused look, repeated it, her expression saying, for God's sake, are you stupid or what? *'Arthur umir',* Arthur's dead. One minute you're standing there with a bag of sweets and tapes your friend will enjoy during the dull hospital hours and the next, he has no use for them whatsoever.

We were in Moscow long enough to attend his funeral. Arthur had been recently and secretly confirmed by the Anglican chaplain and the funeral was held in St Andrew's Church, still partly in use by the Soviet recording company, Melodia. It was a half-ex-pat, half-Russian affair. Mourners were divided down the middle of the church where plastic chairs were arrayed beneath the baffles. His Russian family and friends sat on the left and the British, American and Canadian people he knew were on the right, like guests belonging to bride or groom at a traditional wedding. The service was Prayer Book, but the coffin was open in the Russian Orthodox tradition and at the end of the service, we queued to kiss Arthur's waxy face and lay roses in the ample oak coffin. His widow took photographs, again as if we were at a wedding, and months later, sent some to me in Chester, in a musty envelope that crumbled slightly when I opened it. There were pictures of Arthur, looking peaceful in his comfy coffin and some of elderly Russian men in warm coats and rabbit fur hats, clustered together, friends I assume from his years in Stalin's camps. And there's a photo of you and me singing a hymn, you in the baggy camel coat you wore for years with me somehow tucked under your shoulder. Lydia wrote on the back of that one, '*Kto eta rydom te*?, Who's that standing next to you? That's the question I'm trying to answer.

This morning, I feel a surge of energy and my legs, like those of the girl wearing the endlessly dancing Red Shoes, feel as if they no longer belong to me and I'm being involuntarily propelled to Santiago. I find myself walking in step with a man about my height, we exchange the usual '*Buen Camino*' and there's an immediate tug of attraction. It's a mysterious sensation. He's small, balding and middle-aged and I'm, let's face it, small, overweight and middle-aged, yet there's a magnetism coming from both of us at heart level, and being received simultaneously. He refuses to speak English. My Spanish is rusty but I enjoy speaking it. It takes me back to a day when I was a teenager in rural East Kent. On a day out to Folkestone, I met a crowd of Spaniards on the Number 10 bus and *they were speaking Spanish!* I grew up in a small village and went to school in a sleepy market town. I'd barely seen a foreigner and hadn't connected the Spanish I was learning at school with real people I might meet on a bus. Having a conversation with them thrilled me to such an extent, I still feel the excitement over thirty years later, real people, only slightly older than me, but a million times more stylish and confident, telling me there was a world out there.

Alberto is saying that I really must join him to eat octopus in the town of Melide, half way along today's walk. I don't fancy it. I say I can't possibly eat something with such beautiful big eyes. Alberto looks at me in a meaningful way and tells me it's a requirement on the *camino*, to eat octopus in Melide, that real pilgrims always do. I'm ready for coffee and a cafe presents itself. Alberto skips on, telling me he'll see me in Melide. I'm smiling.

It's a sociable morning. I then get into conversation with a cheerful Finnish man whose name I can't pronounce. I make an approximation by calling him 'Ryanair' which he finds close enough. He gives me a new dimension on the idea of baggage and the body, telling me he's walked the *camino* five times, that his pack weighs ten kilos and that he loses ten kilos every time he does the walk, and puts it on again in the intervening months. This shedding of part of the self on the walk is another kind of leaving, of our own physical selves, burned away as heat and dust as we walk along. Earlier I walk with a couple whose nationality I've been trying to guess since hearing them speaking Spanish, English and French with equal ease. Martin is from Quebec and Tanya is Chilean, they met and fell in love on a beach in Europe. Their love and concern for each other is infectious, emanating out to me and others around us, creating a warmth that is almost tangible, that makes people smile when they see them.

This meeting of people is a cumulative pleasure, each one tells me something new about the world, or simply by coming from, say, Brittany or Sydney or Kyoto, opens windows to new images and ideas. The paradox of us all doing the same thing, yet being individuals that are infinitely variable, reflects the world around us, the same mystery of many yet specific, like the stars in the night sky or flowers in a meadow. And these meetings are nothing much, fleeting five minute conversations, leaving no outward trace, beyond a few vibrations in the air, or the imperceptible change in a wave on a beach picking up the wash of a boat passing faraway.

You often recalled meeting me for the first time on Skyros. We were finishing supper on the first night of the writing workshop. I was impossibly naive, not even bringing pen and paper, unlike your regular students, some attending the course for the second or third time. We ate on a terrace overlooking a steep drop down to the coast and the sea in the distance. Pomegranates dangled from a tree growing out of the low wall and the air was heavy with sage and thyme. I'd arrived earlier than the main group and watched you coming with the other participants down the steps into the centre, hot and bothered, very white-skinned in strangely sporty looking shorts. The group was splitting into little knots of people chatting and I was on the fringes of the one on my table. You were alone on another table looking towards my back. I sensed your gaze, stood up and held out my hand, 'Hello, I'm Victoria Field, I'm in your group.' Later you said my confidence impressed you, how you liked my open face and the way I looked at you. You would sometimes tell people about that moment and quote me, she stood up and said, 'Hello, I'm Victoria Field, I'm in your group.' It's another moment like a photo-graph, except with extra sensory details, the taste of retsina and garlic in my mouth, Mediterranean night scents in my nostrils, warm air on bare skin and you, in front of me, brown eyes so intense they looked black and that something between us.

It wasn't the interesting little tug I just experienced with Alberto but something much stronger, so that now, fifteen years later, recalling it gives me a sense of vertigo. The metaphor of falling feels literally true, falling in love, falling for you, or as I subsequently thought of it in relation to Jung, falling dizzyingly towards my fate.

Later, a group of us went for a drink in the little town of Skyros. I spent that whole fortnight more or less drunk, whether on my first introduc-tion to writing, retsina or brandy, or your reeling me into your world and psyche. The group was a mixed bunch and everyone was setting out their stall, showing off a little, revealing and concealing to this group of strangers. You held court. Now I can see how you were mage-like setting up the dramas that would unfold over the fortnight. At one point, the conversation went to handedness. Cack-handed myself, I'm often in groups that are disproportionately left-handed. You declared your own left-handedness but remarked that you masturbated with your right hand, and asked whether that was true of everyone else. I can't remember any replies but my repressed, thirty two year old self was shocked and intrigued.

You also said, rudely, that there were only two women present you found attractive, me and my room-mate, Susan. I still find Susan totally beautiful. We were sharing traditional village rooms where the crooked walls were hung with sepia pictures of dead soldiers and dusty embroideries and the floor was a trip-hazard of clumsily poured concrete, its craters and ridges barely visible in the half-dark. When I arrived, she was out but her dresses were hanging on nails along a corridor. They were soft and expensive-looking, in natural shades of stone and wood, as if holding the whole of her Colorado landscape. They looked calm and exotic in the stark white and blue of the Greek island sky and architecture, or when compared to my own brash and cheerful holiday wardrobe. I was flattered to be considered alongside this dignified woman with her lovely low voice and it was heartening after the wrench and sadness of leaving my job in Russia a month or so before.

That night was pivota Sitting out in the hot street on hard folding chairs, drinking brandy, watching you, it was as if the planets had been set in motion, the giants of Jupiter and Saturn squaring up to Venus and Mars, and there was nothing, down here on the little bit of earth that was the Greek island of Skyros, I could do about it. I puffed blissfully on my cheap Silk Cuts, laughed at your jokes, smiled at Susan and looked forward to my first writing workshop and my new life after Moscow. It's nothing like that with Alberto. The feeling's in the same domain, but a pale imitation of meeting you. There's no sense of fate, just possibility and the pleasure of mutual attraction.

After my coffee, I walk mostly alone on the way to Melide. The approach is one of the least attractive on the *camino* so far. Blocks of flats and scruffy service roads seem to go on for ages with no obvious centre to the town. I catch up with a Korean woman who seems to be crucifying herself with every step, propelling herself along with two sticks, dragging her weight forward, then putting one foot down tentatively before drawing breath and repeating on the other side. Her face is pale and her eyes are huge like those of an uncomprehending animal being beaten by someone it trusts. I don't know whether she has blisters, or some kind of muscular pain, but every step seems to be agony. She has little English and no Spanish. I mime offers to help her and she patiently watches my sequence of gestures as if I'm playing charades or some other gauche, clumsy Western game. She smiles her beatific smile again and shakes her head.

I carry on and every so often, climbing into the urban sprawl of Melide, look back and it's as if she's in a pool of light on the overcast day, planting her sticks a few meagre centimetres ahead, thousands of miles from home, in a land that might as well be another planet.

Eventually, the long sprawl of Melide's suburbs give way to what's evidently the town centre, with pharmacies and grocery shops and, more than anything, octopus restaurants. *Pulperías* everywhere. There are signs hanging all the way along the main streets, showing merry-looking octopuses dangling freely in space or stylised oceans, or else, less fortunately hanging, missionary-style, over steaming cooking pots. It's lunch time, but I'm still adamant I don't want to eat one of these curiously appealing animals.

I carry on up the main street. As I pass the Pulperia Ezequiel, I hear my name being called, 'Victooooooooria'. Inside, at a long table, are Alberto and his friends, eating octopus. I go in and am soon squeezed in on one of the benches. He introduces me to his walking companions, Vincente and another man from a society devoted to the *camino* in Barcelona. There's a young couple, also from Catalunya, Santiago and Isabel. The table between us is full of wooden platters, small ones for eating from, large ones piled high with cubes of white rubbery flesh, more with rustic bread and there are earthenware jugs of red wine and matching brown tumblers. Everyone's eating with cocktail sticks, spearing the meat then mopping up the juices with bread. The restaurant is cavernous, like a medieval banqueting hall and there's a roar of chatter. In the corners, giant pans are boiling on various ranges where witch-like chefs douse the octopuses. Eventually, I agree to at least taste the *pulpo*. An oily, spicy, tomato sauce coats the white chunk of meat. I'm hungry. My mouth responds involuntarily to the flavour, it's delicious. So I have another, and then another. And, alright, if you insist, a tumbler of red wine. Then, more bread and octopus, its saltiness making me thirsty, so another tumbler of wine. I feel myself getting red in the face, my Spanish is unaccountably more fluent and I can even make jokes so that real Spaniards laugh. And I'm pressed up against Alberto's warmth and entirely comfortable. After the dreariness of the town outside and the asceticism of the *camino* generally, I'm in an oasis of hedonism, and can hear the prissy voice in my head being mocked by the one enjoying herself.

Miro Peregrino is behind us on a table with a group of pilgrims from various countries. As the locals disperse, he starts up the anthem of the Way again, '*Acogenos Senor Santiago, Senor Santiago, acogenos*'. The chorus is repeated over and the pilgrims round the table keep time by banging their wine cups up and down. I love hearing that song and the sound of communal singing and could stay here many more hours, but I heed George Herbert's sound advice to 'drink not the third glass' and decide to be on my way. Alberto and his friends insist on treating me and I stagger unsteadily to my feet.

The next part of the walk is lovely. I'm befuddled but find my way out of the town by an effortful focusing on the sides of the buildings for the little signs. Once clearly on the Way, I relax and enjoy the overcast weather, the dampness in the air, the sense of having eaten and drunk well.

Today, I notice the first memorial to a pilgrim who has died on the Way, a tasteful shrine in the woods, at the side of the path. There are to be more of those in the coming days, and I find them comforting, the words often saying how the person in question died doing something they loved. Passing these memorials, in a state of contentment, I think, yes, if not on this walk but perhaps on one in the future, I'd be happy to clutch at my heart, let out a little dignified shout and collapse, my rucksack curving my back in a strange yoga-like arc. Except for the fact of being a tidy person. It would worry me if I died without returning my library books or answering letters from people I care about. Every trip feels like a mini-death and I'm one of those who neurotically hoovers the house before setting off. Taking the train, or flying is like a reverse birth process, being squeezed into increasingly cramped conditions, especially on a plane, then the emerging into a new world which whilst not nearly as different as places once were, at least smells unusual or has people speaking other languages.

I pass the *albergue* on the edge of town and although it's only early afternoon, see Ryanair sitting on its terrace. He's decided to call it a day and is as full of merriment as earlier. He suggests I stay too but I'm too full of energy and octopus not to want to walk further.

It begins to drizzle and then rain quite steadily. I delve into my pack and bring out the black pouch with the misnamed 'waterproof' inside it. This was the item I economised most on, it's tiny, weighs next to nothing and having borrowed it from my house-mate, I didn't even buy it. It's useless in anything that might be described as 'rain'. Still, it acts a bit like a wetsuit, so at least I don't feel cold when my bra, t-shirt, cardigan, shorts and knickers become sodden as water penetrates the seams and the thin nylon fabric in little more than ten minutes. I don't mind, or at least, not at first.

There are few people on the path. I pass a serene couple who smile a greeting. I think they're Brazilian but I'm not sure, both are tall with dusky skin, black hair and striking, angular faces reminiscent of Easter Island statues. They could as easily be brother and sister as a married couple. They are wearing his-and-hers matching cycle capes, loose fitting so the walker doesn't work up the kind of sweat that I have, yet roomy enough to cover the rucksack and protect the bottom and legs from rain. My ineffectual coat is in stark contrast, tight over my jumper and riding up under my rucksack so my bum sticks out far enough to catch the steady wall of rain dripping from my pack.

The path enters woodland and it's like a sanctuary. The rain patters on the leaves and the layers of humus and pine needles underfoot are fragrant in the moist atmosphere. It's silent apart from the shush-shush of my useless raincoat. The light is diffuse and good for drifting thoughts and day-dreaming. I jump when Alberto comes up behind me. He's dancing along with an ipod dangling from his ears and looks like a wood sprite in his jaunty hat and shorts. We wave at each other and although I think I'm walking briskly, he quickly passes me, dancing to who knows what tune, deeper into the woods.

Every so often the path crosses a minor road, sometimes skirting a house. On one roadside is a table with punnets of raspberries for sale and an honesty box for one euro fifty. The punnets are too big for one person and I dither, but they, like so many things on this journey, seem to be presented as a gift, raindrops shining on them like pearls, large juicy fruits picked by someone hidden away in the farmhouse. They slow me down though. The rhythm of walking is disrupted by having one arm crooked to carry the punnet, the other working its way from berries to mouth, up and down like a steam engine. My co-ordination isn't great at the best of times and this raspberry business slows me down.

I catch up with Mandy and I give her the rest of the raspberries. I can't wait to get rid of them, delicious as they are, what seemed attractive, now a burden. The rain's coming down in stair rods and we start laughing hysterically. We have nothing to worry about, our old clothes are destined to be thrown away, our rucksacks are well-protected and it's afternoon already, so rest and sleep are in sight.

I love Mandy's frankness and we share stories as we walk. She tells me that she's very intelligent and talented musically but physically has always considered herself a klutz, so this pilgrimage was a way of connecting with her body and proving something to herself and the world. She works for a Trade Union in Chicago and knew Barack Obama in his early years. Her special concern is getting decent pay for women in menial jobs like childcare or cleaning. I'm at ease with her, and we laugh a lot, in spite of the rain and a sudden hill to climb through the strange silvery landscape of a eucalyptus forest.

The first time I'd seen a eucalyptus on the walk, it was a thrill but now, seeing acres of them, I feel a primeval revulsion, the same feeling engendered by giant hogweed or the gunnera that's so popular in Cornwall. Like them, it's a plant that seems primitive, too big and out of keeping with the gentle landscapes at the edge of Europe. At the top of the incline, I'm suddenly weary. The alcohol haze from lunch time has dispersed, I'm dehydrated and have the beginnings of a hang-over. And it's still raining. We come into the village of Boente where, for the first time, a priest ushers us into a church. He wants to stamp our *credenciales*, the Pilgrim's Passport. It's bothersome, with all our wet clobber, to peel away the layers, and retrieve our documents, safely protected in various plastic bags. The priest then gives Mandy and me little prayer cards, which means we want to give him some money, which again means a faff, but we are both touched.

It's good to be reminded that the purpose of the walk isn't always to walk. This pause in the church feels longer than it was and takes me back again to Cornwall where St Petroc walked from the north to the south coast, sheltering at night and from the frequent rain in church porches. The charity that ministers to the homeless in Cornwall is named for St Petroc and in medieval times, churches would have been natural places to find sanctuary. We put the prayer cards away with our well-protected *credenciales* and bundle ourselves up into our sodden garments to carry on through the straggly hamlet. I'm slowing down, my legs are leaden and I'm fatigued in the very cells of my body.

Once again, there's an unexpected cafe, just as I feel I can hardly put one foot in front of the other, and will have to rest somewhere, anywhere, even in a wet ditch at the roadside in order to manage the final few kilometres of the day. The cafe is warm, all steamed up like a Turkish bath. There's Mr Ishikawa, also drenched to the skin. He greets me, 'Hello Victoria San' with lots of bowing and claps his hands in delight at my exaggerated bowing back.

There's a group of three young, very beautiful, very wet Czech women, sitting outside, smoking under a canopy that looks as if it will collapse at any moment from the weight of water on top of it. They're downcast and tell me they have only a few days off from their jobs in Madrid and hadn't expected this relentless, murky rain. Their youth and loveliness is disconcerting. Wholesomeness rather than glamour characterises women on the *camino* and I wonder whether that's true of religion in general. Even at the communion rail, it is the male clergy who approach redolent with expensive aftershave, appropriately something by Boss or Only the Brave, their robes snowy or rich red and hands soft and manicured. The women are seldom perfumed, there's perhaps just a hint of Imperial Leather soap, although one woman priest in I know in Cornwall has prettily painted toenails peeping out from her vestments. The role of beauty, or its shadow, plainness, in religion seems to be discussed only in relation to liturgy, music or architecture with ideas of human beauty somehow taboo. The *camino* is full of beauty, natural and architectural, yet young female loveliness isn't a feature, and even unexpectedly here, in this rainy cafe, it's diluted by their miserable expressions.

Revived by hot chocolate, I'm ready for the last walk of the day. The rain eases and the scenery's more picturesque, little lanes bobbing over the top of rolling hills, criss-crossed by low walls with old farmhouses dotting the landscape. The next town, Arzua, isn't far but the received wisdom is that the *albergue* at Ribadiso shouldn't be missed. Down a steep lane, next to a fast-flowing small river, it's a complex of converted farm buildings, renovated to a high standard with grants from the EU. It's one of the municipal hostels which means a modest overnight charge and a grumpy receptionist.

Both Mandy and I ask for lower bunks and get a lecture explaining how it's impossible to give everyone a lower bunk. As the place is far from full, and lower bunks could be allocated first-come, first-served, her reasoning is far from logical. Mandy's ready to remonstrate but I put on a patient face and say, 'Well, only if there is a lower bunk, please don't go to any trouble'. We're eventually given not just lower bunks, but an entire dormitory almost to ourselves, our only fellow resident being Miro, also on a lower bunk.

The bunks are numbered and also very close together, so Mandy is less than a foot away from me, a still and tidy sleeper, on one side and the gigantic form of Miro Peregrino on the other. Like most giants he snores like a train and overflows his little bed.

As I unpack, another pilgrim comes into the dormitory, a wild-eyed dark-haired man. He's been allocated the bunk on the other side of me. When he sees that I'm female and just how close together we'll be sleeping, he turns white. Muttering to himself in Spanish, that he's a religious man but he is, after all, a man, he takes himself off to sleep in another wing of the barn in a bed of his own choosing. The receptionist has the same power of airline check-in staff to decide who should be next to whom and where romance might blossom or conversely, conflict erupt. The proximity of our beds mean that any of us, Mandy, Miro, me or the religious man could easily lean across in the night and kiss the person sleeping next to us. There's a sexiness in the air. Perhaps nearing the end of the *camino* is making us light-hearted in the same way increasing daylight and flowers do in the spring.

As I stroll down to look at the river, I meet Miro coming the other way. He stops to chat and can't seem to help himself, and pins me to the spot by pinching both my cheeks and smiling down at me. I smile back.

The shower block is a walk away across the field and on an industrial scale, with great jets of hot water that pound my tired flesh and bones. There's little in the way of interior finish and parts of the building are open to the elements to facilitate ventilation, letting out steam, and also allowing hundreds of crane flies to come in. Mostly they're motionless on the rough white walls but others do the floaty dance characteristic of those insects as we shower. They freak Mandy out in the next cubicle and she keeps up an entertaining stream of squeals and expletives. I like the oddness of their balletic drifting through the steam as I wash away the fatigue of the day.

Back to the dormitory and on my pillow, I find a carnation. Red, lovely, incongruous, a single flower with all the glamour of a florist's shop has been introduced into this practical world of drying out boots and sodden rucksacks. Alberto. An invitation. A challenge to my celibacy. We're only a night or so away from Santiago where there'll be hotels, beds, rooms with doors and the possibility of intimacy with one other person rather than the random throwing together of several dozen strangers. I brush my hair, apply some lipstick, push the long stem down into my cleavage and set off for the restaurant next door.

Bill and Fergus are there already at a table in the corner talking to the Korean woman I passed struggling to walk. They're drinking red wine and she's nursing a hot chocolate which slowly brings colour to her cheeks. Her sweetness radiates and I feel a physical relief in my own body seeing her seated, with concerned, kind people instead of dragging her wounded legs along. Conversation's stilted but we gather she's a social worker from Seoul. She's come to Spain because she read Paulo Coehlo's allegorical book on the pilgrimage. Apparently, Paulo Coehlo is extremely popular in Korea.

Any attempt at abstemiousness has gone to the wind. The kitchen won't be open for an hour and once in the warm restaurant, bootless and wearing dry clothes, with only countryside all around, there's no temptation to go exploring. So rather than a glass, I buy a bottle of red wine to share and crisps to keep us going. The Korean woman excuses herself to check into the *albergue* and we don't see her again that evening. We have a relaxed dinner of lentil soup, hake and flan. I suppose someone bought another bottle of wine and we begin to talk of faith and God in a way that's seldom easy at home. Surprisingly, religion is not just taboo among my close friends who are mostly secular or vaguely 'spiritual' but it's difficult for many church goers. Over coffee at the cathedral following the Sunday Eucharist, there's seldom any comment on the sermon and the ideas and challenges it poses, just lots of bustle around social events or news of people. God is there at the altar rail where the reredos can dissolve into molten love, but it seems He's not invited to take refreshments with us in the North Chancel after the service.

Bill reminds me more and more of Simon, my Unitarian friend, with his gentleness, wide reading and quickness to deflate pomposity with wit and laughter. I have so many unfinished conversations with Simon and when he passed away, we were estranged. A mutual friend tells me my last letter to Simon was on the top of his pile of correspondence when he died, as if I might have been the next person he would write to. There's always one side of any correspondence unanswered when someone dies and there's sadness or regret depending on which side it falls. Here, in this cosy restaurant on the *camino*, I feel Bill is an angel, in the sense of being a messenger, bridging the gap left by Simon's sudden death. As we talk more deeply, he begins to adjust his glasses repeatedly with exactly the same mannerism Simon had, so it's almost as if I'm there in my dream of Ephesus, conversing with the dead.

Tonight, I dream vividly of other dead people. I see Jo featured in the Guardian in the 'Unsettling Animal Picture of the Week'. He's smiling, surrounded by fish. He was a wonderful cook but I have no memories of him cooking fish, it was always hunks of meat or poultry. Perhaps the fish are grateful to him for not eating them, perhaps they are a Christian image. Like many people I know, he found the Orthodox Church a place where his faith felt at home. At any rate, he looks happy and I'm pleased and amused by the picture. I also dream of Pete, Simon's closest friend, who also died young, that he's living across the road from me in a terraced house. It's great he's nearby, that there'll be the opportunity for more talk about books and plays, for those long evenings we spent smoking dope and laughing. The third part of my dream involves me, my mum, my aunt and my sister tackling a house renovation. All women and a house, the house being me, I assume, and my female relatives trying to sort me out. As I leave the house, I see it's subsiding badly and I can't live there. These images of friends, family and fish seem to be communicating something to me about faith and love, and the house image implies a need to move, not to settle in a wrong place. It's a dream that resolves something, I sleep well and no one kisses me.

On impulse, thinking about the octopus some months later, I google the name of the restaurant. Two reviews from Trip Advisor pop up. 'Excellent pulpo' says one, obviously anglophone, the second, in Spanish, is more elaborate, also rates it four out of five, and talks about having to make a detour to get there. I then google '*Acogenos*', the pilgrim song, and up comes a YouTube video of Miro singing the song at a conference in Poland.

I'm a fan of the internet but still find it disturbing that my memories of a specific hour can be so quickly intertwined with those of strangers, that I can, if I wish, correspond with these people who also ate *pulpo*, possibly from the same plate, drank wine from the same cup in a bizarre communion detached from time and place. We are one body and the appropriately named 'web' or 'net' gathers us like shimmering fish under a starry sky.

Trip Advisor challenges me to rate my own experience. I enjoyed my plate of octopus but I can't categorically say that the pulpo was excellent, nor whether the restaurant merits a detour. The attempt raises other questions such as whether the walk to Santiago was really a five out of five and if so, why? Did I fall for Alberto or think I did? Who is Mandy, really, when she's at home in her Chicago apartment? Are Bill and Simon manifestations of the same human soul? The octopus was succulent in its piquant sauce. I was tipsy and warm. I was eating it in a foreign language, so the meal was nuanced in a way that has nothing to do with food. The gifts of bread and wine, as in all the restaurants on the *camino*, were more than bread and wine. The Spanish review describes the wine in the Ezequiel as 'turbio'. My dictionary gives many meanings for 'turbio': cloudy, muddy, shady, dim murk, mirk, murky, roily, troubled, underhand, thick. All of these adjectives could apply not just to wine but to all these memories, whether of love affairs, a marriage, years spent in Russia, or, indeed a boisterous lunch party, partaking of octopus.

Chapter Eleven

A hard rain

My white t-shirt, which I washed in the crane-fly-filled shower, hangs sodden on the line with a few pairs of abandoned socks and some bright red Y-fronts. It's still pissing down, emphatic rods of rain, making the line droop under the weight of these few items.

I like that t-shirt, it's warm and cool at the same time, with comfortable, three quarter length sleeves but I can't face carrying it with its weight many times multiplied by water to another hostel where it may still not get dry. The wrench I feel leaving it behind in the pretty valley of Ribadiso, is disproportionate and connected to the closeness of the end of the *camino*. I will soon be abandoning the simplicity of this daily routine as well.

The rain can't possibly get any heavier, so I decide to wait a while before setting out and find Mandy too, waiting it out next door in the cafe. After a coffee and a giant croissant, it seems the monsoon has given way to drizzle, and I set off, almost immediately accessing the joy of the past few days. There seems to be nothing more lovely in life than walking along these peaceful lanes on my way to kiss the bones of a saint.

The Way soon leaves the road for a track through conifer plantations that have the same monochrome monotony as those at home, and I wonder whether they date from the same misguided forestry policies. After a while, there are also more eucalyptus trees, their peeling trunks and invigorating scent, foreign in this damp, Celtic landscape. Their scale is still strange but compared to yesterday, magical rather than disturbing, as if there were a herd of elephants grazing in a field usually home to nothing larger than a few rabbits.

I arrive at a hamlet and a local farmer hurries towards me, to tell me, *á propos* of nothing, to 'go to the second cafe' as it has the best Torta de Santiago. He's picked me out, either as a soft touch or else as someone deserving of inside knowledge, but I daren't trust in the existence of the second cafe, so stop at the first, and squeeze in with all the other wet pilgrims, steaming in the cramped interior. All the way along the *camino* there must be second, and even third cafes who do little business, as thirsty pilgrims will always stop at the first one in any village, in case there isn't another.

I feel guilty, as having been specially informed, the least I could do is patronise a second cafe just once. I look into it anyway, thinking perhaps I'll have a drink of water or buy something to take away. But it's grotty, smells of mould and has an unappetising display of fruit on the turn and stale-looking pies. I don't fancy anything fresh, so blaming the farmer who accosted me, I ask for a glass of local *vino dulce* which, at ten in the morning on top of my second coffee, gives me a buzz. I sit outside with a solitary French Canadian man, whom I've seen at various hostels, always glued to the internet. In Ponferrada, he was hunched over the communal computer terminal when I went to bed and was still there in the same clothes and the same posture, when I left in the morning. He is young with an Osama-like beard and is cagey and shy, ill at ease with eye contact and chat. He tells me he came on the *camino* as a homage to a Quebecqois comedian with the brilliant name of Marcel Leboeuf who has completed the Way and written a book about it. I agree to look up M. Leboeuf on You Tube.

Later that morning, I meet the glossy Argentinian girl who passed me over a week before, on my first morning's walking, as I struggled through the suburbs of León. She's still slim and beautiful in head-to-toe lycra but looks softer and is walking hand-in-hand with a large, smiley Dutchman, whenever the width of the path permits. I'm flattered she remembers me and the three of us walk together for a while, getting wetter and wetter in the light but insistent drizzle.

We stop for lunch at a roadside restaurant, geared up for cooking meat on spits over open fires. My tortilla is being freshly prepared and is slow to come so I relax and dry out, enjoying the crackling warmth and cosiness, reminiscent of a country pub at home, and talking to people I haven't seen before. Two French women tell me how they've suffered with bed bug bites, one of them so badly, she's needed antibiotic injections, after which they've stayed only in hotels. A pair of American women from Sacramento, well into their sixties, look incongruous in perfect make-up, extravagant ear-rings and smart headscarves. They're elegant and charming and for all their appearance suggests otherwise, have walked the whole way from France.

The weather clears up after lunch and the landscape becomes more densely populated and the roads busier. I bump into Bill and Fergus in the little town of Santa Irina. They've checked into a small private hostel and are having an early dinner. I carry on, enjoying a sky that, for once, isn't pouring water all over me.

Later, I have only the second feeling of danger on the whole walk, not this time from wolf prints on a moutain, but deep in the woods from a group of workmen laying pipes near an underpass. I suppose strange men, wolves and woods are all mixed up in our imaginations and can trigger similar visceral fears that relate as much to the imagination as mythology. Nothing happens in these woods, but I feel seven pairs of eyes clock me as I realise that I am alone and far from any road or house. As I get closer to Santiago, the path generally feels less benign, perhaps because so many more people are walking it, and there are more towns and main roads nearby.

The men stop working and simply look at me as I pass, their eyes moving up and down my body. My own eyes observe the visual purdah of not meeting theirs but looking into the middle distance as I murmur a '*Buenos dias*'. My body registers their looks with a prickle that creeps across my skin in response to a perceived threat, that cognitively I haven't yet processed. I decide, as with the wolf, that if attack is inevitable, there's be nothing to be done but give up the ghost and not try to run or fight. Their collective gaze follows me along the path and I walk steadily with my hackles up like an animal. Whether it was the drizzle, my determined walk or the fact that they aren't rapists in the first place, none of the men move and, eventually, I hear the sound of them going back to work with their digging and concrete mixing.

I suddenly think of Snow White and the Seven Dwarves and wonder how it would be to find their haphazard house in the woods and to begin dusting it among clouds of bluebirds. I start singing, 'Whistle while you work', turning 'work' to 'walk', remembering the Disney film, the first I'd ever seen at the cinema and the joyful terror of cowering behind the seat when the witch appeared.

I come to another hamlet, Rua, all closed up and with no hostel, at which point, the heavens chuckle and then with a great gust of laughter, let loose a deluge that puts the morning's steady drenching rain to shame. It is as if bucket after bucket of water is being tipped over my head so that rivers run down my spine. The road, on its descent into the town of Arco do Pinho, becomes a torrent so that soon I am splashing ankle deep in a sudden stream. Cars slip and slide to a halt at crazy angles as their windscreen wipers are unable to cope with the relentless rain.

The summer we parted, it rained and rained in Boscastle, the village we visited twice on my first journey to see you in Cornwall, back in 1997. We traced the steps of Thomas Hardy and Emma, visiting the Vicarage where they met and exploring St Juliot's Church where as an architect, the young Hardy had been sent to advise on restoration. I stood, arms out leaning Titanic-fashion into the wind high on Beeny Cliff, astounded at the beauty of the North Cornwall coastline. I fell in love with Boscastle and although you and I never went there together again, it became a place of pilgrimage for me. After moving to Cornwall, I'd regularly go walking there with a friend from Devon and sometimes took visitors to stay at Trevigue, a bed and breakfast in spectacular isolation on the high cliffs towards Crackington Haven.

In 2004, Boscastle was submerged in a freak flood, which, if it had happened at night, would have led to mass fatalities. The disaster that swept away much of the ancient village, took place during the same summer that I was heartbroken in London. With water now well over my boots on the flooding road in Galicia, I wonder what will happen if the rain never stops and the flood starts reaching my knees and then my waist, and I'm swept away.

For Destruction, Water
Boscastle, August 2004

The day our love was over, seventy cars
were swept into the harbour, a helicopter
lifted six stricken children from a drowning roof.

When she moved into our bed, there was only an inch
of air below the ceiling as the woman, gasping,
crossed her lounge and swam up the stairs.

It was unexpected, though a tourist
I don't know from Adam photographed a black wall
of cloud shadowing Crackington sands.

No one cares about the cars
but I can't forget the puzzled eyes of our dog
in the rear window's crazy slide-by.

At first, it was a bit of a laugh,
getting drenched in a downpour showing
no signs of ending – sometimes we want things

to be other than they are – sea-spray to come vertically,
a river where once was a road – to see ourselves afresh
through another's eyes. A skidding bus,

raindrops big as sweets make us feel more alive.
I kept going to church, mumbling the words
like that farmer stuck at the top of a tree,

reciting prayers he didn't know he knew.
I packed box after box
and you wept at the sight of the van

while all the shoes from Clovelly Clothing
and a Coke machine for good measure,
washed up useless on beaches in Westward Ho!

Summer visitors took shelter in the Wellington Hotel
where a local recalled the other river, sixth-sensed
its hurtle and dash down the village street,

shouted *Everyone out!* It was a miracle nobody died
when mud filled every crevice of the deserted bar.
Now it's all been rebuilt, some say improved.

No, no one actually died.

No people died in the floods, but something died in Boscastle. The
bridges were replaced and the buildings were reconstructed as facsimiles
of themselves using insurance money, but the ancient woodland of the
Valency Valley, where the burst river banks swept away trees, still looks
devastated several years later. It simply isn't the same.

In Arco do Pinho, I can barely open my eyes as the rain pours from my
hood over my forehead and down my face. I fail to pick out the small sign
for the municipal hostel I am aiming for, and end up at the private hostel
on the other side of the road, which I recognise from the photo on my
little leaflet.

Standing, drenched, at the reception in a puddle of my own creation
that spreading in all directions over a pristine floor, I feel I am in a surre-
alist happening. The hostel, incongruously, is Japanese-themed. I look up
to what, behind the ordinary Spanish High Street facade, is a giant glass
atrium complete with a blossoming cherry tree and the sound of
recorded birdsong and plinky music. Like a bad joke, a water feature
tinkles in a corner. It is immaculate and the dormitories are a series of
cleverly designed interconnecting spaces so that no one feels crowded
and it is possible to see only a few other beds at a time. The colour
scheme and everything about the place is calm and beautiful, as if I've
followed a wet and arduous yellow brick road to somewhere over the
rainbow. I thank whatever quirk of fate led me to miss the municipal
hostel with its no doubt lumpy beds and smelly bathrooms.

I shed my wet things and attempt to stuff my boots with paper but
have no expectation they'll be dry by the morning. The hostel's theme of
beauty continues when I meet a pair of Italian women in the bathroom,
blow-drying their hair. Both are beautifully made-up, wearing designer
jeans and are busy styling the swishing long straight hair of models. I
haven't seen a hairdrier since leaving Cornwall and stand, like a nineteenth century peasant seeing a train for the first time, gormless, with my
jaw dropping at their improbable standard of grooming. Yes, says one,

Joanna-Lumley-like in her graciousness, she has carried the hairdrier five hundred miles from St-Jean-de-Pied-de-Port and her comment challenges me with an unspoken 'why not'? Of course, all of these things are simply a question of priorities and these women are, after all, Italian and Italy, if it stands for anything, is famous for elegance and style. And why not create a pilgrim's hostel in Galicia with all the attention to detail characteristic of a tea ceremony in a Japanese garden?

I cross the road to the Barabic bar. It is jumping, literally, with crowds of pilgrims trying to see one another over the many heads. I am thrilled to see so many of my *camino* friends, excited and smiling in this heightened, almost-there, just one more day's walk until we kiss the relics and jump-for-joy atmosphere. It is a vision akin to painter Stanley Spencer's Cookham scene of the Resurrection, where the graves around the village church are flung open and all the people you think you'll never see again, materialise. There is Manuel whom I'd left behind at the high hostel, greeting me like a long lost friend, Mr Ishikawa, looking bemused in his flapping overcoat, Isabel and Santiago, the young couple who laughed at my jokes in the *pulpería*, the Swiss ladies who dressed Bill's poisoned foot, and, and … There is a mass of waving and embracing, of lifting glasses to toast each other across the noisy room, loud music and a bank of computer terminals where people email and skype, the hiss and clatter of coffee machines and snake-hipped young waiters squeezing through the crowds as they emerge laden from the swinging doors to the kitchen.

I usually hate crowded bars, but this feels like the antechamber to the cathedral in Santiago, a preparation for our encounter with St James, and makes me think, perhaps heaven is less a celestial banquet than a laughter-filled bar where the atmosphere is young, even if many of the clientele are old or middle-aged, where people love each other simply because they are there and they've been walking the same path, with no knowledge of past sins of commission or omission.

On the *camino*, we respond to each other in the unconscious way of creatures, perhaps even, given our exertions and clothes that are washed less often than at home, picking up on each other's smelly secretions like dogs, sensing, without needing any facts, yes, he or she is part of my tribe. Even though I know nothing about them, there's something in their smell, their posture and the way they look at me in just the right way. Like a dog, we need no more information than the simple presence of a person to determine whether they should be greeted with licks and wagging tail like a long-lost friend, or else given a wide berth.

Alberto spots me and weaves his way through the densely packed crowd, joining me as I sit on the plastic banquette at the back of the room and, with ostensibly no choice, given the lack of space, presses his thigh firmly against my thigh and his shoulder against my shoulder. What do we talk about? I haven't a clue but given the noise and my ropy Spanish, it can't be in any depth. I am conscious of my hair being in his face and feeling glad it was newly washed, even if not elaborately blow-dried in the style of the Italians. He spends some time recommending the hotel where he and his friends will stay in Santiago, reasonable and central, but I should telephone ahead to book if I want to stay there too. He writes down the address and phone number and carefully draws a little map, all the while pressing his wiry body against my soft one, his tongue appearing frequently like a lizard's between his white shiny teeth. I hadn't thought ahead to Santiago, or at least not beyond the cathedral. I want to keep my options open between staying in a hotel or hostel, to decide later between comfort and privacy or conviviality and privation.

Someone at the bar yells his name, and he stands up and I feel my body release and expand into the space he vacates. He reminds me again of the name of the hotel and folds the piece of paper into the palm of my hand, emphatically pressing down with his index finger.

My dog-sense told me I liked Mandy the instant I met her. My thinking human self finds her increasingly interesting and likeable the more we talk, so I am pleased she is in the bar, even though she is staying in a different hostel. We eat together, a farewell pilgrim's supper as she is making an early departure from Santiago. The proprietors could easily, given their captive clientele, cut corners and serve a meagre dinner. But everything is delicious, with a choice of courses and I tuck in voraciously, my appetite attenuated by my earlier drenching, to garbanzo soup, salmon and boiled potatoes and, just to show how trendy and up to the mark the bar is, tiramisu. The meal makes me suddenly sleepy and I leave soon afterwards to sleep deeply in the Japanese dormitory where birds sing in the distance, water trickles constantly over precisely placed pebbles and the air smells of new wood and soap.

Chapter Twelve

The Mount of Joy

I am back at the Balabic for breakfast early the next morning. It has an altogether different atmosphere, with just a dozen or so quiet customers dotted around. Outside, it is still raining, but gently, and inside, we are hypnotised into silence, heads tilted upwards, by a bank of TV screens showing the news, then a weather forecast. When the glamorous presenter points out the unmistakable symbols for torrential rain across the entire Spanish peninsula, we all laugh, a little hysterically. My boots, anyway, are still sodden, squelching out water in cartoonish bursts at every step.

Then someone behind the counter switches the sound off the televisions and puts Bob Marley on the music system, so that the talking heads of journalists and politicians bob not quite in time to 'One Love'. Many of us customers too begin to sway and bob our heads a little, involuntarily, over our breakfasts. It's the kind of sentimental song that can, in the right context, quickly move me to tears, in the same way I'm hopeless in a church if the hymn is 'Morning Has Broken' or if someone plays 'Somewhere Over the Rainbow' at a funeral. In the Barabic bar, on the last day of my pilgrimage, I am in a state of heightened emotion and wired for tears. Bob Marley is the first catalyst. As I make my way to the loos to compose myself, my waiter from last night jumps out from behind the computers, like a jack-in-the-box, calling to me, 'Cuckoo, cuckoo!' and bobs down again. It is so silly and sweet that I cry even more at the same time as I can't stop laughing, setting the tone for the emotional roller-coaster of the day.

Someone once told me that tears in church are a sign of blessedness. Margery Kempe, of course, had no doubt and rated her general satisfaction with life in terms of how much crying she'd done on any particular day. Science suggests crying is a healthy way of excreting harmful neuro-transmitters, as long as the tears are from joy or grief. Apparently, tears generated by onions or hayfever don't have the same cleansing effect. I'm always relieved to see someone else crying in public and wish tears were as normal and acceptable as laughter. The two, of course, are so close physiologically and psychologically that one always eventually morphs into the other. Or sometimes it's hard to know what's going on emotion-ally – the waiter's jokey behaviour combined with Bob Marley's timeless injunction to feel alright, makes me giggle and sniffle simultaneously.

I am prepared today for a twelve mile slog through the suburbs, in a mirror image of the first part of the walk through urban León, but once I've cleared the town, I am once again strollling through conifers and eucalyptus, in an increasingly familiar landscape.

Inevitably, I catch up with Clive and Hamish at the first hamlet with a cafe. They stayed at the posh, private hostel with Bill and Fergus, and said it was comfortable but pricey and also, I suspect, quiet and predictable compared to the packed bar last night and the odd temple-like Japanese hostel. Their seemingly-impregnable twosome has turned into a trio. A young Bulgarian woman in the same hostel has taken a shine to Hamish. She is dark-haired and dramatic-looking, and hangs on his every word in rapt, and slightly uncomprehending, admiration. Hamish is still limping slightly, and she walks beside him, gazing up solicitously as he progresses with his lopsided gait.

I surprise myself by feeling jealous of her. I'd assumed it would be my place to fall for Hamish, if I hadn't learned he was married and that his wife was a bosom pal of Clive's wife. I like everything about him, from his intelligence, his confidence in his own business and enjoyment of success, to the way he talks enthusiastically about food and France. I am especially impressed by his cheerfulness in the face of what must have been gruelling and disappointing days, suffering so much pain and injury early in the *camino*. I feel the Bulgarian isn't 'playing the game' but of course there is 'no game', or at least not outside my head. And much as I've taken to Hamish, there is now Alberto's clear invitation folded into my money belt, to join him in Santiago, at his hotel. My new definition of a hotel no longer has anything to do with comfort or services but the fact that they have rooms and doors. Doors, those brilliant inventions that improve so dramatically on curtains, that not only keep prying eyes at bay but offer the illusion of John Donne's little room being an everywhere.

The path is less picturesque when it skirts the Santiago's airport, to which many of the pilgrims will soon be returning by bus or taxi for their journeys home. As if on cue, just as I am reflecting on the long distances covered by the Brazilians, Koreans and Canadians, I find myself walking again with Linda, the Australian, who, now free of any luggage and well-rested in comfy hotels, is moving along easily and in high spirits. She tells me about her work serving drinks and snacks on the Australian railways. Her husband, who is still a considerable distance ahead, eager to 'get the job done', is employed in the same position. We talk about the economics of trolleys and the variety of people she encounters, the stress and difficulty manouvering inside trains on bumpy tracks. It seems in Australia, her job is a civil service one, with perks, pension and pay that allow for trips round Europe. My interest is genuine. The trains heading east or north are an important aspect of life in Cornwall. The finer details of the catering and other aspects of their running make all the difference between pleasure and misery on long trips up-country.

I am sure you weren't the only passenger suffering 'smoke-rage' when the ban came in and trains were regularly delayed by smoking passengers getting out at every stop and refusing to be hurried back on. Soon, the platforms were policed and many of you smokers simply stopped travelling by train, five or more hours to London being just too long. There's a lot of camaraderie and catching up with friends and acquaintances on trains between Cornwall and London or Bristol, and often, before the smoking ban, you'd alight in Truro stinking and merry from being crammed into the one carriage reserved for smokers, where someone produces a bottle of wine, and all kinds of interesting encounters and reunions occur. That convivial carriage of people united in their common craving was not dissimilar to the gatherings for the pilgrim's supper, where like the smokers, we're united by our unreasonableness in the face of a rational world.

Soon after the airport, the Way follows a chain link fence, dividing pedestrians on the *camino* from the trunk road and roundabouts. It goes on for a few hundred metres and is increasingly densely covered with ribbons and wooden crosses. Many of the crosses are improvised out of twigs or branches, others are well-made, seemingly specially brought to be left on the fence. People have also tied on scarves, bandages and hand-kerchiefs, even a pair of tights, and there are photographs too in various states of faded decay.

The repeating crosses, in their thousands, are the most moving, seeming to say, like rows of war graves: loss, loss, loss, loss, loss, loss, *ad infinitum*, loss. The cumulative effect is ultimately numbing. When you and I drove to the town of Albert and toured the area around the Somme, visiting the many carefully tended cemeteries and chatting to the fresh-faced young Canadian couple who looked after the Newfoundland Memorial, I felt a strange disconnection. The Canadians were glad to speak English and share their frustration at how, in France, shops shut for lunch and in the evenings and explained how Newfoundland wasn't even under the dominion of Canada during the Great War. We weren't part of any of the English-speaking tour groups sitting at communal tables in the hotel restaurant, of historians, veterans or just the interested general public, almost all men, and there was no structure or articulated purpose to our trip. We had a map, your rich general knowledge, First World War poetry anthologies and our private thoughts.

For some, who can name loved ones who died there, such a journey would be a form of mourning or a way of seeking closure, even a pil-grimage, which in its modern secularised form, is any journey imbued with meaning. It wasn't a journey I would ever have made if it hadn't been for your enthusiasm – twentieth century history is one of your passions. I was happy to have a holiday in a beautiful corner of France and learn more about the First World War but I found myself uncom-fortable with what might be described as a kind of recreational grief. The emotion that welled up in me, thinking of those strangers and the horror of life in the trenches, felt general and inauthentic, as if I was watching a well-crafted film where the director had palpable designs on the audience. The rows of beautifully tended graves evoked feelings that seemed clichéd and didn't touch the deepest part of me in the way, say, the keening of the sow did, in her stable next to my rented rooms on Bodmin Moor.

We sought out a particular grave, that of an officer ancestor of a friend of yours who'd mentioned it when we'd said where we were going. There was some satisfaction in being able to engage specifically with one grave as our eyes slid over the serried ranks of white memorials. I knew that three of my maternal grandmother's older brothers had died in World War I, boys in their late teens from a pitifully poor household. Their graves are dotted around Ypres somewhere and the words 'cannon fodder' seem especially appropriate for Nottinghamshire peasants. Perhaps those would have prompted some genuine pity in me.

I thought a lot about 'Testament of Youth' on that trip, the story of the life of Vera Brittain that I'd seen serialised on television when I was sixteen and then read, carefully several times. Bruno Bettelheim writes in 'The Uses of Enchantment' of how fantasy and fairy tales enable children to make sense of the world. For me as a teenager, the factual content of 'Testament of Youth' fascinated me for similar reasons. Vera's tragic losses, including both a fiancé and beloved brother, the horror she witnessed as a nurse at the front, her thirst for knowledge and ability to shake off the expectations of her parents for the life of an Edwardian young lady, filled me with admiration and also some envy of the way world events gave Vera a clear purpose and mission.

How much the great events of history impact on us has much to do with the chance circumstances of date of birth. Your father's age meant he missed active service in the Second World War but other wars took place in your family as your older sister took up with American and Australian soldiers based in Cornwall. You return often in your writing to the tensions and excitement of those days. Your own National Service enabled you to learn Russian, a gift to your emotional and writing life, and not only that, but you studied in Bodmin, so you could go home for weekends. Harry survived the Death Railway but his childhood was blighted by the trauma his own father suffered at Gallipoli, two generations of men both cruelly used in wars. My motor mechanic Grandad, sent to Italy to fix jeeps, not only got a medal but the kudos of being able to say with Cockney pride, 'When I was out in Italy ...' for the rest of his life without having to bother again with 'abroad'. He and my Granny found everything they needed at home in their little bungalow. All these people's wars are as individual as these crosses made from tied up twigs along the fence.

We were both thoughtful on that drive through France and we alternated studying the graves and monuments with picnics in rolling countryside and strolls through peaceful villages alive with birdsong and early summer flowers, trying to imagine the lanes as they would have been almost a hundred years ago.

I emailed you recently, asking, 'When was it we went to the Somme?'. You replied, 'Began July 1st 1916. Brits had 60,000 casualties on first day, including 20,000 killed'. 'No,' I emailed back, 'When did *we* go to the Somme?'. You replied that you had no idea. That small exchange says so much about history and memory, the difference between the momentous and the easily forgotten. A number equivalent to today's population of Truro is killed in a single day, and several decades later, you and I sit on folding chairs not far from the site of the slaughter, eating crusty bread and drinking wine from plastic glasses on a roadside verge full of cow parsley and ladies smock. One event is the subject of thousands of books and memorials, the other simply forgotten, the ordinary subsumed to the extraordinary. Our brief email exchange, reminds me of a joke about gender differences, where a man declares that his wife makes all the small decisions, like where they live and which school the children go to, whereas he makes the big ones, such as whether we should join the euro or invade Iraq. For you, 'we' not only refers to Britain as an agent of foreign policy but to a Britain way back in history, whereas for me, that 'we' is just the two of us, outside history, on holiday in Picardie, in a year neither of us can identify.

The various agencies involved in that area of France have transformed devastation into calm beauty, inchoate pain into order and decorum. This stretch of the *camino*, in contrast, is scruffy. It feels like walking through a graveyard, not a manicured one but a raw makeshift affair as if people have been buried hurriedly or, where there were so many deaths, it's impossible to deal with them in an orderly way. It has echoes of the vast cemeteries outside small South African towns, where every Saturday, priests are busy from dawn to dusk burying people who've died of AIDs, the mourners mostly the deceased's children and parents, vulnerable young and elderly thrown together in loss and poverty.

I've no idea why the fence on this particular stretch of the Way has become such a shrine to the crucifixion. Perhaps, it just takes one person to tie on a cross for private reasons and others follow. There's a similar fence in Italy covered in padlocks on the coast path at the Cinque Terre. The stretch is known as the Via del'Amore and the padlocks symbolise eternal love. Couples buy them in hardware shops in the villages, attach them to the fence and throw the keys into the sea. Maybe it's fences that are provocative, like the one at Greenham Common in the 80s, with its decorations of socks, poems and family photographs.

In Cornwall, the many holy wells are festooned with rags and ribbons, harking back to a romanticised pagan past. There are no crosses and no obvious images of suffering. Perhaps it's a cultural difference, to do with the British stiff upper lip or fear of the body. The Spanish seem to tell it how it is in the paintings of Zurburán, Velasquez and the graphic sculptures of the seventeenth century, all unflinching in their depiction of the mortification of the flesh. Nails hammered through the hands and feet of Christ, deep lash marks from the whip and the way the rough rope minutely shreds the top layers of skin and flesh, are not suggested at, but depicted with anatomical precision. The skin is shown breaking and layers are peeled back so that bright fresh blood emerges through the black congealed scabs from wounds of previous days. I dare you to look, the paintings seem to say, I dare you to be honest about suffering. I read somewhere that the Greenham women tied used sanitary towels to their hated fence. This seems akin to religious art of Spain, connecting the body not just to the spirit but to politics, challenging ideas of what it means to be an embodied human being or to be part of a religion with a mortal body its heart. Unwanted secretions and raw flesh, alongside, in the case of the paintings, accurately depicted, beautiful draping fabrics, belong together. Vera Brittain cleaned and dressed shrapnel wounds as she grieved for her fiance and brother. The old man in Ponferrada finds meaning in gently ministering to pilgrims' blistered feet. The visual shock of damaged flesh wakes us up, to a spirituality that's challenging, and the reality of our vulnerable bodies. It seems an important counterbalance to images of sunlight through trees, rainbows and candles which can lull us to spiritual sleep.

Our pilgrimage is a pilgrimage because there are bones of a saint to be reverenced at the end of it and we've walked here as flesh and blood, some even with bleeding feet. Everyone's making a physical effort even if the degree of bodily suffering seems to be luck of the draw. Thankfully, I haven't seen any of the self-flagellation or other mortifications that characterise penitents in Andalucia during Holy Week but perhaps that isn't qualitatively different from the walk the rest of us are doing.

Like a clever theatre director, the *camino* seems to know when and how to change the mood. Just as the valley of death seems to be going on too long and resistance is creeping in, it stops and changes direction. I climb a few more hundred metres, happily chatting to Clive, Hamish and the Bulgarian and we are soon up on the Monte de Gozo, the Mount of Joy, drinking Coke from a makeshift refreshment stand and sniggering over silly double entendres.

This is the point from where in medieval times, pilgrims would have seen the towers of the cathedral standing high above the plain below, sur-rounded by a small walled medieval town. Now, of course, the cathedral is just one building in a vast urban sprawl of factories, ring roads and apartment blocks. It's still thrilling to pick out its distinct sillhouette in the old town, now only a few miles away. We hang around a bit on the Mount, taking photos and climbing to the very top, chatting, and somehow hesitating to set off on the final descent into the town. As in the bar in Arco do Pinho, there is a feeling of light-heartedness and 'gozo', the Spanish word for enjoyment, pleasure, joy and delight.

A Scottish man joins me as I walked through the suburbs. He is on holiday in the city and has walked up to Monte de Gozo out of curiosity, to see the pilgrims coming in. He wants to know about the Way, asking me questions I am incapable of answering coherently. The general 'What was it like?' is an impossible one, although I've often been asked it of walking to Santiago, and indeed, of being married to you. He is a friendly, thoughtful person and on another day, I would have enjoyed his company but today, I am relieved when he takes the hint and hives off down a sidestreet, leaving me alone with my thoughts.

It's the first big city I've been in since the start in León and I am struck by how, unlike in the villages and small towns, pilgrims are now in the minority on the pavements. For the past fortnight, pilgrims have formed a constantly flowing river of rucksacked people, and yet here, they are outnumbered by shoppers, motorists and office workers. They are just dots amongst people in clean clothes and normal shoes, not wearing rucksacks but carrying a handbag or briefcase, or nothing at all. The locals have that slightly closed expression of people going about their daily lives rather than the wide-eyed gawp of a newcomer seeing a place for the first time. It is noisy and like Crocodile Dundee, I am struck by the quanitity of everything – people, cars, restaurants, shop windows. Passing a shoe shop, I am amazed that so many styles of shoe can exist in one small place and am suddenly worried by my reaction. I've only been walking for twelve days which doesn't seem long enough to turn me into a Martian seeing a normal European suburb as if for the first time.

I've read about how common it is for people to have psychotic episodes when visiting Jerusalem as a tourist. They lose touch with reality, as if simple proximity to places made holy by centuries of conviction can turn a brain. Perhaps such a reaction in a place as potent as Jerusalem is logical, just as my seeing the suburbs as if for the first time, is a kind of revelation. Having grown used to moving between one pair of boots and one pair of sandals, that shoe shop seems crazy, an expression of excessive and strange priorities. I write this, having just downsized in quite a drastic way, and yet I can still count a dozen pairs of shoes that I own without leaving my chair. Perhaps I need to walk for longer to get a more effective dose of reality,

Santiago is arranged in concentric circles and the modern part suddenly gives way to its medieval heart. The traffic-filled dreariness and the banal shops stop at the city walls. There are still plenty of people and things on sale but there is the hush of pedestrianised streets and the shops are smarter, selling jewellery or tasteful souvenirs. There are also the ghosts of the hundreds of thousands of earlier pilgrims. Margery and Egeria appear either side of me, one weeping uncontrollably, the other almost imperceptibly rolling her eyes. Without quite knowing what the building is, I wander down some steps and enter the cathedral through the north door and am immediately stilled by the size, the ornateness, the majesty and sheer over-the-topness of the building. St James in his roccoco splendour, dominates the centre, with his massive Disneyesque face and a gaze that follows me around the building.

I am here. I am here. What do I do now? Where do I go?

There are essential errands, to collect my *compostela*, to check in somewhere for the night, to call or email to say I've made it, have a shower and get changed, attend Mass, visit the shrine. And, when I've done those things, to start a new life. I'm paralysed and sit for a while, arms embracing my rucksack on my knees like a child and stare into the impassive face of St James amid his glitter and ceramics. It's a rerun of my stint musing on the mountainside, eating bread and banana, not thinking in any logical way but allowing my thoughts to drift like clouds, high up and far away in a clear sky.

Eventually, I come to, and identify my first task as claiming my *compostela*. I soon find some arrows on the sides of buildings, pointing to the office that issues them and feel again in the safe hands of the *camino*. It's too soon to shed the habit of looking for arrows to follow and for months to come, I'll be alert to anything painted on a wall or a roadside. The office is in a medieval building, up a few flights of well-worn stone stairs to where a row of officials sits behind low tables, in front of filing cabinets, bookshelves and other office paraphanalia. There are a few other people queueing. The couple in front of me are asked where they've walked from. 'Germany!', they reply proudly. I feel a sense of let-down. Why haven't I walked from Germany like this radiant young couple? When it's my turn and I hand over my *credencial* with its brightly coloured stamps, I say 'León!' loud and clear and inwardly add 'this time', resolving immediately to make another pilgrimage in 2013, in the spring of my 50th year, and to walk for a month at least.

The various stamps in my *credencial* are examined and the woman official nods and writes my name on the pre-printed *compostela*. She hands it to me and says 'Well done, Janet!' I must look blank as she repeated her congratulations. The *compostela* has reversed my given names to Janet Victoria. It makes me smile – perhaps it happens to everyone but I often seem to be called by the wrong name, usually Veronica or Virginia and people tend to add an s to my surname, even carefully engraved on a silver plaque I once received as a prize. More than once, I've arrived at a conference to see myself listed as Victoria Wood. So now, I'm Janet, my aunt's name, a Scottish name and not that common amongst my age group. It is appropriate, I suppose, for a new start in life.

And I'm officially indulged. If I were Roman Catholic, my *compostela* would give me partial remission from any temporal punishment that might be due. It seems I've got off lightly as I've arrived in Santiago physically unscathed. Perhaps a more equitable way of accounting would be to issue stamps for blisters, bad knees or dodgy backs rather than for miles walked. The image of the French woman and her weeping feet floats in front of me like one of the polychrome statues in the cathedral, merging with Picasso's weeping Dora and Margery Kempe. I imagine handing the official a plastic bag full of used tissues and handkerchiefs as evidence of a pilgrimage well done.

The alleys and side-streets are full of signs saying 'rooms' and I check some of them out. The buildings are romantic and clearly ancient but the bedrooms on offer are bleak, sparsely furnished, some with put-you-ups instead of proper beds. Perhaps they are appropriate for pilgrims, but they lack the warmth and camaraderie of bunks in a dormitory. None of them appeal and I stroll back to the vast square in front of the steps leading to the Portal of Forgiveness and the west door of the cathedral. The square is full of life and activity. Locals stride across it purposefully whilst tourists and pilgrims wander around, holding aloft cameras and phones. Still undecided between a hostel or hotel, I go back inside the cathedral and sit down again in the nave.

Suddenly there's a hand on my shoulder. It's Alberto, who's spotted me through the crowds. He's shaved and showered and changed into fresh clothes and smells nice, of some kind of Spanish soap. We exchange Holas, and Que tals and Muy biens. He tugs at the gold cross around my neck and asks if I've repented of my sins. I answer that it's none of his business and then his fingers follow the chain around to the back of my neck and bury themselves in my hair, twisting it and pulling gently. He asks if I've checked into a hotel yet and I tell him, no not yet, then he says, follow me. I have just a moment of indecision but then I do. We make our way through alleys and side streets and into a tall thin building with a small sign saying hotel outside. The staircase is steep and the room, on the fourth floor, is warm and tranquil, simply furnished, with a double bed with a white lace counterpane and ample pillows. A tall window frames a view of roof-tops and as Alberto closes the curtains, rain begins to fall, leaving diagonal silver lines across the panes and pounding a tattoo on the roof tops. Although I thought I'd long forgottten, in Jane Hirshfield's words, my life opens again, 'into an afternoon of darkness and rain, into what the body carries at all times within it and starts to remember each time it enters the act of love' .

No, that didn't happen. I'm not ready for Alberto and when he approaches me in the cathedral, I am friendly but gently remove his hand from my neck, squeeze it and say, I am heading back to the hostel. A shadow of disappointment crosses his face but then he smiles, kisses my cheek and promises to email.

Leaving the cathedral again, I see the famous parador stretching the length of the north side of the square. It's the oldest hotel in the world, built on the orders of Isabel and Ferdinand, los Reyes Católicos, as a huge pilgrim's hostel in 1492, the same year Christopher Columbus set sail. It's magificent, with a giant archway and doors leading into a central courtyard, all renovated to a standard of perfection. I walk closer and see uniformed doormen turning away tourists, telling them the building is a hotel and therefore private, and they can't come in with their gawping, riff-raff ways. Immediately, I want to stay there, to be able to walk freely through that magnificent entrance. All those nights on soggy mattresses and my decisions to forgo hotels during the previous two weeks, persuade me I've done enough penance.

I do some sums in my head. Modest hotels would have cost me 40 euros or so, less the amount I'd spent in hostels, somewhere around 10 euros each night, mean I still have a few hundred euros I could easily have spent. I decide the maximum I can pay for a night in such a palace is 150 euros, any more and I won't enjoy the experience. I can't imagine rooms will be available at that price, the obvious luxury and the historical significance makes this one of the world's most desirable hotels, but having caught the eye of a doorman and seeing him about to inform me that I can't go in, I meet his gaze with a confident smile and continue walking, so that instead of barring the way, he steps forward to open one of the huge glass doors. Cinderella will go to the ball.

The receptionist looks me up and down. I try to appear respectable and somehow look clean. She consults the computer, a colleague and looks a few times at the clock. It's getting on for three and the likelihood of walk-ins will diminish as the afternoon wears on. Eventually she smiles, *Bueno*, we can let you have a room for 150 euros including breakfast. I nearly burst into a loud rendition of 'Walking back to happiness' and positively skip behind the bell-boy who insists on carrying my rucksack up sweeping staircases and along a corridor to the most beautiful room I've ever slept in. It is full of antiques and paintings, the mullioned windows frame the towers of the cathedral against a grey sky, the bed is firm and made up with an inviting combination of feathers and blankets. The curtains, carpets and upholstery are lush reds, vibrant and pristine. And the bathroom. Oh.

I spend a while exploring the room, looking at where, in a different incarnation, I might have hung my designer clothes, picking up the kit for polishing the shoes I don't have with me or pressing the trousers that were beyond pressing. I examine the expensive and tasteful array of toiletries. I do a double-take on finding a hand-written note on a pretty card saying, 'Your room has been prepared for you by Victoria.' Thank you, Victoria. You're welcome, I reply.

No, of course I don't stay at the parador, the prices are over two hundred dollars a night and it would feel completely wrong to be a pilgrim and spend such a sum on luxury. Of course, I can't resist Alberto's attentions and after all the puritanical privations of the previous fortnight, the prospect of an afternoon making love.

The hours blur into evening and somewhere around ten o'clock, Alberto and I head out to find some supper. The whole town is full of celebrating pilgrims, a roar of conversation emanates from every establishment we pass. We are waylaid, seeing Bill and Fergus drinking beer in a tapas bar.

We join them and I order sardines and croquettes. Bill and Fergus are staying in a hotel they'd booked from Canada and tell us how nice it is. I am embarrassed that I can't remember where I am staying, nor how much it costs – just that it is a pretty hotel in an old building, not far from the centre. Alberto fills them in. Mandy has already left for the airport, she is under time pressure to get home to Chicago, and I am sorry not to have said a proper good bye.

My supper couldn't have been better. The sardines are firm, bright silver and flavoured with lemon and olive oil, the croquettes, soft and yielding in the centre and the red wine, rich and oaky. Or possibly, it is all ordinary, but I have a heightened appetite not just from the *camino*, but from the feeling of coming alive, being connected, engendered by the long hours of skin on skin, that makes everything delicious. It feels like a fitting last supper. I order a bottle of a different wine, some *vino de verano* which is light and up-cheering and the four of us toast the *camino* and journeys to come.

No, that's not true. The whole point of the pilgrimage is to lay my marriage to rest, not to have a fling with a man I know nothing about, casual sex that would soon seem sordid and irrelevant. I need to be alone, to reflect, to pray and where better to do that than in the quiet, comfortable luxury of the parador? They offer a much reduced price as it is a late check-in, so I decide to indulge and take a long bath, cleansing both body and soul, as I float happily in a slick of fragrant oil. Then I doze briefly on the heavenly bed. I can see the point now of a bleak room in a cheap pension with an uncomfortable put-you-up. If I was in one of those chilly bare rooms, there would be no temptation to sleep all afternoon. Here, the high, firm bed is a siren, saying to me sleep, sleep, sleep and I have to summon huge will-power to get up and go out.

Eventually, I get up, brush my hair and put on lipstick, retie my boots and make my way out to the square, zigzagging down the parador's many staircases and landings, looking at the views framed by the windows, some out to the cathedral, others into the ancient, complicated court-yards.

The city is fascinating and I have the rest of today and all of tomorrow before getting on the sleeper to Madrid. There are services in the cathedral, museums, shops, letters to write, and of course that wonderful bed to sleep in. I can go back to my room, just for the pleasure of walking in and out through those magnificent doors and making the long trek to my corner of the vast building, feet cushioned on expensive carpets, fine art in every direction, but I'm waylaid by seeing, who else, but Clive and Hamish drinking beer in a tapas bar.

I join them and order a late lunch of sardines and croquettes. They've already collected their secular versions of the *compostela* and purchased, sensibly, special tubes to carry them home in. They are staying in a little hotel they've booked from England and tell me how nice it is. They've made it, reached Santiago in the optimistic time frame they'd set them-selves, and in spite of seeing them zip into the distance after our conver-sation on the second day, I've kept pace, and arrived at the same time. They ask where I'm staying and I'm suddenly embarrassed at my extrav-agance and won't tell them the cost of my room but I learn that another pilgrim is also staying at the parador – the grumpy German woman I walked with through the orchards beyond Sarria. I would challenge her to find anything in that palace that can be described as 'shit' or 'total shit'.

My lunch though, really is shit. The sardines are soggy and flavourless, the croquettes have been refried and have the texture of cardboard and the red wine is bitter with tannin. Or possibly, I've lost the heightened appetite of the *camino*, engendered by long hours of walking, that makes everything delicious. I have a sense of anticlimax. I order a glass of a different wine, some *vino de verano* which is light and up-cheering.

Then, we see a prostitute come into the bar, case the joint and success-fully pick up a pilgrim, from North America, judging by his clothes, who was sitting alone at a table. Rubbish food and sex workers must have been a feature of Santiago a thousand years ago and suddenly the sordid, commercial side to the whole pilgrimage enterprise makes itself apparent. I suppose my horrid lunch is a kind of penance, off-setting my luxurious accommodation, assuming of course, that God deals out our fate according to some kind of accountancy principles.

No, it wasn't like that at all.

We watch the other pilgrims in the bar and see a young man, from North America, judging by his clothes, slip his arm around the shoulders of one of the Czech girls I'd seen drenched in the cafe on the way to Ribadiso. She nuzzles her head against his shoulder, and he pulls her closer. Good food and pilgrims copping off together must have been a feature of Santiago a thousand years ago and this cheerful, secular side to the whole pilgrimage enterprise, makes itself apparent. Alberto slips his arm round my waist and I wonder what I've done to deserve such pleasures and whether at some later stage, I'd need to do penance, assuming of course, that God deals out our fate according to some kind of accountancy principles.

Alberto has to leave early in the morning to catch his train home to Barcelona and I see him moving like a shadow in the pre-dawn. 'Don't get up', he tells me as he leaves, rucksack on his back and ipod round his neck, and I continue to doze until, eventually, I hear the chimes of the cathedral clock striking nine. I shower, brush my hair and put on lipstick, retie my boots and run down the steep, stone hotel staircase, looking at the views framed by the windows on each landing, some out to the city, others into the courtyards.

I spend my last day mostly in the cathedral, in the company of Margery and Egeria, going to Mass three times, queueing to embrace St James, saying my prayers and wishing I was still walking. Margery cries most of the time and Egeria makes copious notes in her notebook in her fluent, but I understand from later commentators, 'slipshod and tedious', Latin. She tells us, she is planning to produce another volume of her travels for her Sisters, but this time, she will focus on her return to 'the ends of the earth', rather than her journeys east to Jerusalem and away from it.

A nun emerges before each Mass to teach us the responses so by the time of the daily Pilgrim's Mass, they are familiar to me. The cathedral begins to fill an hour before it's due to start, and soon every seat is taken, mostly by pilgrims, but also elderly Galician women, and tourists who look too smart to have walked here. In a quieter re-run of the gathering in the Barabic bar, pilgrims are waving to each other, embracing and smiling hellos.

During the Mass, a list of those who have gained their *compostela* is read out, sometimes by name, but today, and I suppose, now on most days as the numbers continue to increase, by number from each country. Pilgrims lead some of the prayers in their various languages. The nun conducts us as we sing our responses, the event is solemn and celebratory at the same time.

I'm engrossed and have completely forgotten about the *botafumeiro*. The Galician translates it as 'smoke-expeller' and it's the largest censer in the world. It's only swung on high days, or when someone has given a large enough donation to the cathedral, as the incense is so costly, so I hadn't dared hope to see it in action. It's a genuine surprise when eight red-robed *tiraboleiros*, 'pullers of the smoke-expeller', move forward and begin to heave on long ropes, attached to pulleys high up and out of sight. The giant thurible, which was sitting in front of the altar, looking like a medieval dalek, starts to swing and bounce as it's jerked upwards. Organ music plays loudly, and the eight men bend down and heave some more, up and down, like bell ringers, and then the thurible, belching smoke like a living dragon, begins to sway from side to side, describing an increasingly huge and dangerous arc, north to south and back again across the cathedral transepts.

The air fills with incense and the throbbing, soaring sounds of the organ and a thousand hands, holding phones and cameras are lifted, flashing above our heads. People weep and embrace each other and the thurible bounces threateningly at the end of every oscillation, like I used to as a child, going too high on the swing. It picks up speed with every circuit, reminding us how it weighs 80 kilos, apparently, with an additional 40 kilos of charcoal and incense, and travels at almost 70 kilometres an hour, and, how it could, if those gentlemen in red, in charge of the ropes get it wrong, take out many dozens of worshippers in one go.

Egeria writes frantically, describing the priests' vestments, the psalms and the singing nun. Margery's crying is drowned out by the music and I feel my spirit lifting with every crazy swing of the censer, then slowly coming down to earth as it eventually slows down, the music subsides and the cathedral echoes to applause from the thousands of worshippers. And St James in his roccoco glory watches over us all, our tired feet on the holy earth where his luminous bones were buried, and our many, many faces lifted towards him like a field of stars.

Epilogue

Alberto, Vicente and their friend
Annique and Alicia
Antonio
Beverley and Bill
Bill and Fergus
Clive and Hamish
Carolina
Geoffrey
Heidi and Trudy
Isabel and Santiago
Mr Ishikawa
Jon
Kim and Kathleen
Lars
Linda and Paul
Luciano
Mandy
Manuel and David
the other Manuel
Marie Jose
Martin and Tanya
Miro
Roberta, Titty, Petra, Griet
Ryanair
Sylvine and Marcel
Tim and Jane

I make a list of all the people I encountered on the *camino* in an attempt to lift my mood as I sit at Madrid Airport, sulking. I am tired and grubby from the sleeper from Santiago where I've been bitten by bedbugs for the first time on the trip. But the immediate cause of my grumpiness, is a wrap I've bought at one of the food outlets. It sounded, from its description on the menu board, delicious. Served up in a plastic box, it is vile. Something hot has turned the lettuce into brown slime and everything tastes of cardboard. I am sitting in an entirely plastic world in the hellishly large terminal, breathing artificial air and close to tears.

I go back to the counter to complain but the man says, not unreasonably, that I've eaten too much of it for a refund, I should have brought it back sooner. But it's horrible, I repeat, like a mad woman, getting shriller and more insistent as I recite my litany of disappointment. Look at the lettuce, it's vile. Yes, he agrees, it is, but you should have told me earlier, I can't do anything now. I refuse to back down, as if I need absolution for some dreadful sin. The man behind the counter also won't budge but I can see him looking around the virtually empty terminal for support, should the crazy *inglesa* turn violent.

Our arguments often reached the same impasse. Like the arguments between most couples, they repeated themselves. I would complain and you, not unreasonably, would say that's how I am, you could have left earlier. But in a spirit of optimism – after all, the menu had promised something delicious – I carried on eating.

And then, I met someone who wasn't on any menu at all. I embarked on a extra-marital affair of my own, only to discover I was soon intoxicated by this handsome, kind, practical person I'd found. I'd heard you say so often that affairs meant 'nothing' and even though I didn't believe you (otherwise why bother?) I decided to take a risk myself. The outcome was that I became happy and alive and nicer to you, stopped recriminating and asking you questions. My confidence and *joie de vivre* returned and I didn't need constant reassurance of your affections. The downside for you was that I no longer wanted to be close or to share your bed. I began to wake up, and ask myself what kind of life I really wanted.

Standing at the counter in the airport, I similarly come back to my senses and asked myself what exactly I want. A replacement wrap would be as unappetising as the first, even if the lettuce wasn't soggy. And I am no longer hungry for food. I suppose I want the man behind the counter to do something about my unhappiness. Back in those heady days, when I first went walking with my new friend, or sea swimming late at night, naked in moonlight and phosphorescence, I wanted you to put your foot down and say, enough is enough, stop it, let's fix this strange, crooked animal that is our marriage. But you didn't. Instead you saw it as a green light for your own affairs and possibly the beginning of the open marriage you claimed to want. Finally, the marriage-animal became so profoundly misshapen and unhappy, the only option I could see was a mercy killing. I came back from those dark days in Bloomsbury and made an appointment with a solicitor, using only one or two of the tissues in the giant box on her desk.

The sandwich man then shifts his position, understanding, I think, that my mad complaining is nothing to do with the wrap but some kind of grief for all the things I've lost. If I were to identify one thing from our years together, it would be our shared bed that symbolises so much. Sex with you was interesting, to say the least, but what I grieve for is that warmth of bodies pressed together, the way we slept, both still and quiet for hours on end, in the bedroom at the end of the long thin house, only occasionally disturbed by a sudden start in a dream, or our lips meeting casually in the night as if there were only one mouth, his and hers an arbitrary distinction. The bedroom like the prow of a ship, with its triple aspect windows seemed to sail through the night. A breeze was usually blowing gently, lifting the orange curtains I'd bought, so that every morning, the room was filled with a dappled apricot light. Your weight on the mattress or your heavy arm flopped over me, our regular breath, the warmth under the duvet and your scent which wasn't – as people would insist – just cigarettes, the fresh air, the snuffle of the dog in her basket and the purr of the cat creeping onto the bed, combined to create a bliss that was as simple and wordless as sleep.

And there in Madrid Airport, I was missing more immediately, the simplicity of my recent existence, walking the *camino* on a sunny day in Galicia, surrounded by apple trees, long grass and empty villages, the air full of angels.

Something gives, and the sandwich man breaks into a broad smile and I laugh at my own ridiculousness. He offers me a sweet from a bowl on the counter, presumably kept there for children. It is a large chew in a lurid wrapper. I accept it and feel at peace.

I am back in the real world. The next stop is an overnight at my sister's in London where my little nieces enjoy the fans and castanets bought in Madrid. I am up early the next day and then straight out that morning on a plane to Avignon for a dear friend's sixtieth birthday. I've posted ahead her present, a party dress and ludicrously high gold wedge sandals.

At the party, I dance all night and nearly fall in love with a small dark man of sixty, but am saved by learning his much younger girlfriend is at home expecting his first child. Then, I sleep intermittently but deeply, for a full twenty four hours on white linen sheets, next to another guest who also spends most of the weekend in bed. She is a beautiful Canadian singer and psychic, with terrible jet-lag, who tells me spooky stories whenever we wake up at the same time, imbuing my dreams with supernatural images.

On my return, from Nîmes to Luton, I have another fight in the airport when the security guard confiscates the little stainless steel flask I used for water along the Way. It has already passed as hand luggage through three airports and is clearly completely empty.

Again, like a mad woman, I repeat my case over and over again and the man just shrugs and says, no, I can't have it back. Are you really going to throw it away? Yes, he says, yes. The little flask given to me by my Russian Orthodox friends and carried from fountain to fountain two hundred miles across Spain? Thrown away? Yes, he says, and gives a final full stop of a shrug and walks behind a barrier so I can no longer catch his attention.

Something else gone, like the books, our bed, the breeze through the house, our talk and laughter across restaurant tables on all those islands, our arguments, my tears, all the moments that make up a marriage and the love that leads up to it. Everything passes – and every step on the Way took me further from you and nearer to the eternity that awaits us all.

The Thiepval Memorial in the Somme commemorates over seventy thousand soldiers who went missing in battle and so were not given a proper burial or tombstone. The lists of names are giddying, as if every single person in Truro and Falmouth and all the surrounding villages were individually listed. There are blanks, though, amongst the names. These are where the names were of those men whose bodies were subsequently found and identifed and who were then given the proper rites of passage and an individual memorial. The authorities along the *camino* are also assidious keepers of lists. From the elaborate registers of the hostels along the Way to the medieval office that issues the *compostela* certificates at the cathedral, every pilgrim's name is written down over and over again. As time moves on, the names on the Thiepval Memorial will become more abstract, the lists less immediate to those who peruse them, looking for some kind of hook of meaning. How different from the anguish in Anna Akhmatova's 'Requiem' where, describing the queues of people looking for news of loved ones outside prisons in Stalin's Leningrad, she writes, in your translation, 'I would like to call you all by name, but they have lost the lists'.

Somewhere, in the lists held by the Registry Office in Truro, our names are side by side, and again in the Magistrates Court of that same small city. They are no longer together on envelopes, Christmas cards or invitations, that rhythmical pairing of two names now only echoing when people reminisce about the past. My own list of pilgrims met along the Way is full of arbitrariness, the single ones, the couples, the pairs or trios of friends, the ones I can picture clearly, the ones whose faces have already faded. I would like to call you all by name, but time passes and memory is fickle.

And in a way nothing has happened. The guns weren't firing and nobody died. I just plodded along part of the *camino*, not doing anything out of the ordinary nor even going particularly far. Someone else was barefoot. Another, with a beard down to his navel, was leading a donkey. I hear of someone's friends who walked with a guitar and accordian and gave impromptu concerts along the Way. I read blogs by people who've walked more than a thousand miles or who have photographed every church en route. At the beginning of my own walk, when I still thought two hundred miles or so in twelve days was impressive, I met an elderly couple going the wrong way. They'd walked to Santiago from Oslo and were heading home again. There's always more, further, harder, different. Some people were walking to do penance for terrible sins or to grieve tragic losses, whereas I was just in a mid-life muddle. Yes, a marriage had failed, but were the guns firing?' No, they weren't. No, neither of us actually died.

But something changed. My faith deepened. The veil is increasingly thinner and I see through it more often. Sometimes, kneeling at the high altar during the Eucharist, the reredos turns to molten light and I feel the presence of God as a force, both wind and water, and neither, against my face and body so that it's hard to stay upright. It happens too outside, when I'm walking alone and light breaks through clouds and falls, like a slab of beaten metal onto the sea, or when the sun catches dimpled jewels of dew on cobwebs the length of the coast path. These are all, of course, just tricks of the light but I'm increasingly interested in the trickster behind them.

Margery Kempe puts this mixture of doubt and certainty better than I can. She writes that there are people who think 'revelations are deceits and illusions, and therefore it is not appropriate to give credence too readily to every stirring but wait steadfastly and prove if they be sent from God. Nevertheless, as for this feeling of this creature, it was the very truth, shown in experience, and her fear and her heaviness of heart turned into great spiritual comfort and gladness'.

Jesus turning water into wine at the wedding in Cana is a story that has been explained to me since primary school as evidence that Jesus liked a good time and being nice to people. After the pilgrimage, though, I understand the parable for the first time. Once certain that the eternal is real and that there is a loving order, all water is already wine. The cold gush from the tap, a clean glass, a few ice cubes from the miraculous freezer ticking away in most kitchens in the Western world, give a drink that is as pleasurable as a gin and tonic (well, almost). Similarly, the air on a cold winter's morning, makes me feel merry in the same way champagne can. A photograph of a robin on the cheap Christmas cards I've bought in Boots, reveals, in its grey, brown, red and pink feathers, the bead of its black eye and the spindles of its legs and feet, the whole, bewilderingly wonderful, ordered madness of the natural world.

'Why have enough when you can have too much?' jokes an old boyfriend who enjoys his food. And looking around me, I feel I've got too much, a surfeit of love and pleasure, a healthy body, a past and a future, a head full of ideas not to mention access to books and the web for the ideas of others. The water of my discontent has turned into a wine of gratitude – whether it's simple plonk or a particularly good vintage, I've no idea but it makes me good humoured, a bit pink in the face and happy that, whenever the end comes, I'll easily drift into a satisfied sleep. 'The past is prologue'. The first chapter begins. I retie my boots, pick up my rucksack and step out of the house, as an act of faith, not of hope.